P9-BIG-547

Problem Regions of Europe

General Editor: **D. I. Scargill**

The Lower Rhône and Marseille

Ian B. Thompson

Oxford University Press 1975

Oxford University Press, Ely House, London W.1

Glasgow New York Toronto Melbourne Wellington
Cape Town Ibadan Nairobi Dar es Salaam Lusaka Addis Ababa
Delhi Bombay Calcutta Madras Karachi Lahore Dacca
Kuala Lumpur Singapore Hong Kong Tokyo

Filmset by BAS Printers Limited, Wallop, Hampshire
and printed in Great Britain
at the University Press, Oxford
by Vivian Ridler, Printer to the University

Editor's Preface

Great economic and social changes have taken place in Europe in recent years. The agricultural workforce in the west was halved, for example, during the 1950s and 1960s. This unprecedented flight from the land has made possible some much-needed reorganization of farm holdings but it has also created problems, not least that of finding uses for land in the highlands and elsewhere where it is no longer profitable to farm. Closely related is the difficulty of maintaining services to a much diminished rural population or of providing new kinds of services for the holidaymakers who increasingly buy up rural properties.

Contraction of the labour force has also taken place in many traditional industries. The coal-mining industry alone has shed two-thirds of its workforce since 1950. The resulting problems have been especially serious in those mining or manufacturing districts which have a high level of dependence on a single source of employment—a not uncommon result of Europe's industrial past—and the efforts of those who seek to attract new industries are often thwarted by a legacy of pollution, bad housing, and soured labour relations.

Quite a different set of problems has arisen in the great cities of Europe such as London and Paris and in the conurbations of closely linked cities well exemplified by Randstad Holland. Here are problems due to growth brought about by the expansion of consumer-orientated manufacturing and still more by the massive increase in office jobs which proliferate in 'down-town' business districts. The problems are economic, social and political, and they include the effects of congestion, of soaring land values, of the increasing divorce of place of residence from place of work, and of the difficulty of planning a metropolitan region that may be shared between many independent-minded local authorities.

The problems resulting from change are not passing ones; indeed they exhibit a persistence that amply justifies their study on an areal basis. Hence the *Problem Regions of Europe* series. The volumes in the series have all been written by geographers who, by the nature of their discipline, can take a broadly based approach to description and analysis. Geographers in the past have been reluctant to base their studies on problem regions since the problem was often of a temporary nature, less enduring than the 'personality' of the region but the magnitude of present-day problems has even resulted in the suggestion that regions should be defined in terms of the problems that confront them.

Certain themes emerge clearly when the basis of the problem is examined: the effects of a harsh environment, of remoteness and of political division, as well as of industrial decay or urban congestion. But these have not been examined in isolation and the studies that make up the series have been carefully chosen in order that useful comparisons can be made. Thus, for example, both the Mezzogiorno and Andalusia have to contend with the problems of Mediterranean drought, wind, and flood, but the precise nature of these and other problems, as well as man's response to them, differs in the two regions. Similarly, the response to economic change is not the same in North-East England as in North Rhine–Westphalia, nor the response to social pressures the same in Paris as in the Randstad.

The efforts which individual governments have made to grapple with their problems provides a basis for critical assessment in each of the volumes. For too long, solutions were sought that were piecemeal and short-term. Our own Development Areas in Britain provide a good illustration of this kind of policy. Of late, however, European governments have shown an increasing awareness of the need to undertake planning on a regional basis. The success or otherwise of such regional policies is fully explored in the individual *Problem Region* volumes.

When it was first planned the *Problem Region* series was thought of as useful only to the sixth-form student of geography. As it has developed it has become clear that the authors— all specialists in the geography of the areas concerned—have contributed studies that will be useful, not only for sixth-form work, but as a basis for the more detailed investigations undertaken by advanced students, both of geography and of European studies in general.

D.I.S.

St. Edmund Hall, Oxford

Contents

The Lower Rhône region provides a fascinating contrast with the Lower Rhine, analysed in an earlier volume in this series (G. R. P. Lawrence, *Randstad Holland*). Both rivers rise in the Alps; both flow through highly industrialized and urbanized middle courses, the Lyon–Saint-Etienne–Grenoble complex reproducing on a smaller scale the industrial complexes of the Ruhr and Middle Rhine; both involve impressive power schemes; both are active corridors of movement; and both terminate in extensive deltas. It is in their lower sections that the most striking contrasts emerge, however. The Lower Rhône cannot match the Lower Rhine as a waterway, the level of urbanization is much less impressive, and port development is only now assuming a scale which resembles in embryo that of Rotterdam–Europoort. Clearly, the lesser economic stimulus of the Mediterranean as compared with the North Sea–Atlantic routeway, and the lower economic development of the French Midi as compared with the great conurbations of the Rhine hinterland largely explain this disparity.

The scale of this disparity is, however, being reduced. The Rhône valley has become a highly active axis of movement, served by motorway, piplines, and electrified rail, while the Rhône itself is being rapidly improved as a waterway. Power schemes have spread downstream into the lower reaches of the valley. Marseille, like Rotterdam, has expanded from the confines of its initial port site in order to develop a new port/industrial complex. An urban revival is spreading the built-up area onto previously unused or agricultural land. A region, until recently beset with the problems of an agricultural society and struggling for mastery over a difficult (if potentially rewarding) environment, is now learning to accommodate an urban, industrial society. Thus begins a new chapter in the long history of the Lower Rhône region.

The process of regional transformation

Few European regions have been so thoroughly transformed in the course of the last few decades as has the Lower Rhône region. Until after World War II, the Rhône was an obstacle, its capricious flow hindering navigation and at intervals inundating the valley floor. The delta area was an economic cul-de-sac, sparsely populated and with a very low level of economic activity. To the east of the delta, the port of Marseille, whilst highly active, relied on staple items of trade serving national demands rather than animating the regional economy in its immediate hinterland. To the west of the delta, traditional agricultural methods held sway, viticulture enjoying an almost monocultural importance. The uplands flanking the valley and delta also had retarded agricultural economies and were subject to high rates of rural depopulation. With the exception of Marseille, the urban structure consisted of small or medium-sized towns, essentially market centres, under-industrialized and tending towards somnolence. The impression conveyed in 1945 was one of a region with a glorious historical past, a present which was marking time, and an ambiguous future.

The problems confronting the region were both natural, deriving from an environment prone to extremes, and man-made, resulting from retarded economic development coupled with a neglect of investment, especially in industry. At the same time, it was clearly a region where the forces of nature could be turned to very great advantage. The powerful flow of the Rhône could be harnessed, from Switzerland to the delta, to provide abundant energy and improved navigation as well as water for irrigation. The same fierce heat that scorches the region during the summer drought could, given irrigation, make the agriculture one of the most productive in Europe. The advantages of a hot sunny climate, vivid natural scenery, a rich cultural heritage of Roman and medieval monuments, and, to the west of the delta, vast empty coastlands, conferred on the region an enormous potential for tourism at a time when Europe's tourist industry was poised for its greatest-ever period of expansion. In short, in the immediate post-war period, the Lower Rhône was a region with an outstanding potential, but a potential which could be realized only by a sustained effort of modernization and an integrated approach to resource management.

Almost thirty years later, the Lower Rhône region must be viewed in an entirely new perspective. No longer is the Rhône an obstacle to progress. Instead, the multiple use of its water and energy resources has given rise to one of

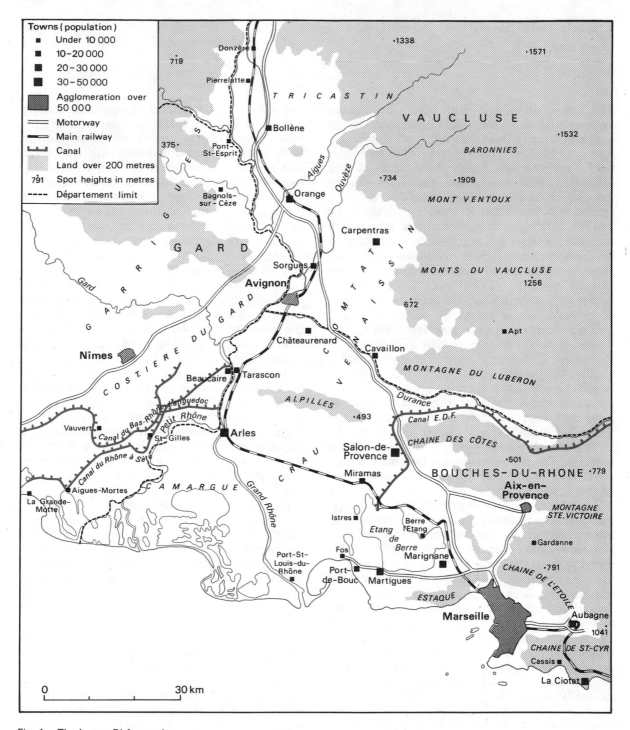

Fig. 1   The Lower Rhône region

Europe's most striking integrated developments. The electrification of the railway, the laying of oil pipelines, and the construction of a motorway network have converted the valley from a simple corridor to an axis of movement and activity of potential European significance. On a smaller scale, the basin of the turbulent Durance, with its alternation of flood and drought, has been transformed into a stable sub-region, the river supplying power and water for irrigation and urban uses. The once desert-like Crau plain has, by means of irrigation, been transformed into a zone of pioneer viticulture, fruit-growing, and rich pasture, whilst the Camargue now gives France almost complete self-sufficiency in rice production. The port of Marseille has broken out of its constraining mountain chains to develop specialized outports, initially on the Etang de Berre, and more dramatically in the last decade, on the virgin site of the Gulf of Fos. This latter expansion brings to an end the isolation of the delta area, for the Fos-sur-Mer project is one of the most ambitious port and industrial schemes in Europe. To the west of the delta, water from the Rhône is being employed to turn monoculture of the vine into intensive fruit- and vegetable-growing on efficient farms, whilst the formerly barren coastline is now punctuated by modern tourist complexes.

This striking progress, compressed into such a short time span, does not imply that the Lower Rhône region has solved all its problems. Ironically, while striving to solve ingrained problems, the new developments have called into being a fresh set of difficulties. For example, the extension of irrigation into former areas of viticulture calls for a revolution in farming practice and a reorganization of marketing methods. The implantation of Fos-sur-Mer on the borders of the Crau and the Camargue has brought fundamental environmental changes to a unique natural area meriting the highest ecological protection. The completion of hydro-electric power stations, with their related industrial zones, calls for changes in employment patterns and urban functions.

Although giving a welcome boost to the level of economic activity in the region, the new developments also raise numerous questions as far as the future is concerned. Thus, whilst the port complex of Marseille has taken on a fresh lease of life by virtue of its new annexes, the future of the original port nucleus at the heart of the city is uncertain. Subjected to the modification of colonial trade since Algerian independence, the unfavourable effects of the closure of the Suez Canal, and a general decline in passenger liner traffic, Marseille is witnessing an inevitable concentration of traffic in the specialized annexes, including Fos, that are equipped to handle bulk imports of petroleum and minerals as well as container traffic. Similarly, although the Rhône power schemes have greatly improved inland navigation, the waterway is still of only limited significance owing to the lack of adequate connection with the Rhine system, which effectively denies it a hinterland of continental scale. A further doubt concerns the relationship between the development of the Lower Rhône region and the adjacent upland and mountain fringe. Planned development has been concentrated along the valley corridor, in the delta, and on the plains to either side of the delta. No comparable growth has taken place on the mountain fringe of the Cévennes, the *garrigue* uplands of Languedoc, or the high plateaux of Vaucluse. Undeniably, this reflects basic inequalities in resource potential, but little recognition has been given to the long-term implications of progressive depopulation of the peripheral uplands and increasing congestion and environmental stress in the lowland core.

Perhaps the greatest uncertainty attaches to the future evolution of the Fos-sur-Mer project. Many commentators have termed this scheme a gamble, although admittedly an audacious one. Vast capital investment has already been committed, and to justify the expenditure several objectives must be attained. Manufacturing industries must be attracted to Fos if the port is not to be just a break-of-bulk and primary processing point. The scale of port construction demands that Fos must develop an extensive hinterland if it is to compete successfully, not only with north European ports, but also with other expanding port/industrial complexes on the northern shores of the Mediterranean such as Genoa. Moreover, Fos is more than just a port/industrial complex. It is the centrepiece of a zone of new urbanization on the Crau plain and around the Etang de Berre. This poses a double challenge —that of achieving a satisfactory urban environment in spite of unsightly and to some extent pollution-prone industries which are difficult to hide in the monotonous physical landscape of the Crau plain, and also that of successfully integrating this urbanization into that of the existing agglomeration of Marseille within the context of a metropolitan plan.

In spite of the very substantial progress made in the Lower Rhône region since the war it still remains a problem region, but the character of the problems has clearly changed. In the past it was the physical environment that posed the most severe problems, but technology, in the form of flood control, water storage, irrigation works, power schemes, and innovations in crop production and farming methods, has largely overcome the physical obstacles to economic progress. The new problems are basically of an organizational nature. The region has to adapt to the new conditions brought about by technological change, transport development, industrial and urban expansion, and the resultant ecological adjustments. In the view of many observers, solutions to these new problems can be found only in the context of an enlarged field of action for planning purposes—the 'Grand Delta' of the Rhône. This 'super region', embracing the Rhône itself, the Alps, the eastern and southern margins of the Massif Central, and the Mediterranean façade is formed by uniting the present planning regions of Rhône–Alpes, Languedoc, and Provence–Côte d'Azur. Thus constituted, the 'Grand Delta' accounts for ten million inhabitants and one-fifth of France's national land area. The concept of integrated planning for such a large area belongs to the future and to the realm of long-range strategic planning. The problems analysed in this volume characterize a much more restricted area, and further discussion of the 'Grand Delta' concept is deferred to the close of the text where it forms a fitting conclusion.

Definition of the Lower Rhône region

Throughout most of its extent, the geographical unit of the Lower Rhône region poses no problem of definition as there are clear physical and functional boundaries. The general outline is that of an inverted letter 'Y' and it is only at the southern extremities that the boundary is uncertain and transitional.

The northern limit is defined as the Donzère defile (Fig. 1), where the Rhône flows through a narrow gorge at the point where the Massif Central and the Alps approach each other most closely. North of Donzère, the climatic transition from the Mediterranean regime becomes pronounced, with resultant changes in both natural vegetation and crop range. In economic terms, the area north of Donzère falls within the orbit of the Lyon–Saint-Etienne–Grenoble metropolitan complex. Important valley routes converge on the Rhône, notably those of the Isère and the Saint-Etienne coalfield furrow, and industry becomes progressively more prominent within the corridor itself. The south-eastern limit is less precise as there is no marked climatic transition other than that induced locally by relief, and the limit coincides with a zone of great structural complexity resulting in alternations of basins and chains with a limited development of through routeways. A line drawn several kilometres east of an arc from La Ciotat to Gardanne and Aix, and projected to the Durance valley at Cadarache, approximately defines the section of Lower Provence with a high level of activity, looking to Marseille and to the Rhône corridor, as opposed to interior Haute Provence. The latter has a much lower level of economic development, fragmented urbanization, and impeded communications.

The south-western limit is even less precise, for here the Rhône lowland coalesces with that of Bas-Languedoc with no significant topographic break. A line drawn along the Vidourle river to the western edge of the delta serves to delimit that portion of the huge Languedoc plain which is being increasingly drawn into the Lower Rhône and Marseille orbit. It must be stressed that this is an unstable border rather than a fixed limit. In one direction, irrigated agriculture watered by the Rhône and encouraged by experience in the Rhône valley is spreading into Languedoc towards Montpellier. In the other, the planned expansion of tourism intended to reanimate the whole of the Languedoc coast has penetrated the Rhône delta zone. Since the general trend is for increased integration between the eastern sector of the Languedoc plain, within the hinterland of Nîmes, and the Lower Rhône region, it follows that the boundary adopted must be a relatively arbitrary one.

The limits adopted above define a region of two million inhabitants with certain common problems. But it is essentially a composite region, in which the Rhône corridor serves as a main artery, the Marseille complex an outlet and metropolis, whilst the network of medium-sized towns represents the foci and relay centres within the urban and transport systems. The situation and function of these towns display great variety, from centres of small agricultural *pays* such as Cavaillon and Carpentras, and strategic river-crossing points (often leading to twin-town development) such as Avignon–Villeneuve and Tarascon–Beaucaire, to centres situated at the junction of contrasted regions, such as Nîmes. The area defined does not form an administrative unit, falling within three *départements* and parts of two planning regions. It does, however, represent a coherent unit from the point of view of development problems, a unit within which the most ambitious attempts at integrated planning in France are to be observed.

The mosaic landscape of the Comtat Venaissin   I.N.R.A.

Sub-regional components

The Lower Rhône region may be subdivided into five main components: the Lower Rhône valley, the delta, the Marseille–Aix–Berre complex, the Lower Durance valley, and the eastern section of the Languedoc plain, each of which may in turn be subdivided into sub-regions of greater or lesser distinctiveness.

The Lower Rhône valley

The Rhône enters its plain course south of the Donzère defile, this extending as a broad valley lowland as far south as the Alpilles range, which marks the northern limit of the delta zone. After the alternation of small plains and constrictions which characterizes the middle Rhône between Lyon and Montélimar, the valley broadens out into a wide plain, in large measure due to the convergence on the Rhône of broad left-bank tributary valleys. On the right bank, the Cévennes foothills and the Garrigues maintain a more or less continuous upland front. By contrast, to the east of the Rhône, wide lowland embayments alternate with tongues of high plateau: the Diois, Baronnies, Ventoux, Vaucluse, and Lubéron ranges. Within this upland framework, the Lower Rhône valley consists of a roughly triangular lowland, divided into two segments of contrasted character. To the north of the Aigues, the continuity of the plain is broken by enclaves of *garrigue*. This is Tricastin, the northern marchland of Provence, where viticulture and

olives predominate and few towns are present. The completion of the Donzère–Mondragon power scheme in 1952 has, however, transformed the western section of Tricastin. Irrigation has permitted an intensification of agriculture on the Rhône plain based on orchards and market gardens. Industrialization has taken place at Pierrelatte and Marcoule in the form of nuclear research and plutonium enrichment, and in the special steels plant at l'Ardoise. Construction work on the power scheme and the subsequent growth of industry has stimulated the development of the small towns of western Tricastin.

South of the Aigues, the remainder of the Lower Rhône valley comprises the Comtat Venaissin. This is the garden of Provence, a landscape of minute holdings in which the small fields are protected from the fury of the mistral by cypress and cane hedges in a dense mosaic of intensive agriculture. On the broken terrain of the right bank viticulture is dominant, but on the left bank centuries of draining and irrigating soils which are not always highly fertile has produced an agricultural landscape of astonishing opulence. Fruit growing and market gardening predominate in an agricultural system which is highly developed both in production methods and marketing. Irrigation is supplied by a network of canals from the Durance and the produce is marketed through a chain of towns equipped with *marché-gares* to ensure rapid transit. Avignon, Châteaurenard, Cavaillon, Carpentras, and

Orange are the main centres of a marketing system in which co-operative organizations play an important role. Avignon is the main administrative, commercial, and cultural centre and has a very large tourist trade. The southern boundary of the Comtat is formed dramatically by the Alpilles range. This chain of limestone mountains is not high, only 387 metres at its maximum, but the vigour of the folding and severity of erosion make for spectacular scenery. The summits consist of barren karst but orchards, olive groves, and vineyards cover the flanks.

The delta zone

In broad terms the delta zone may be divided into two halves, one which is too wet (the Camargue) and the other too dry (the Crau). In fact, this oversimplifies a very complex environment in which minor variations in relief, drainage, and soils produce striking changes in land-use, but in which the modifications brought about by man give the impression of his having virtually overruled natural conditions.

In physical terms the Crau is the 'dejection plain' built by the Durance in its former course east of the Alpilles. It is built up of coarse pebbles which until recently supported a semi-arid steppe fit only for sheep grazing and military manoeuvres. Hydro-electric works have diverted the Durance to this former course, and the landscape of the northern and eastern margins has been transformed as a result. Sheep now graze irrigated pasture and high quality hay is marketed. Formerly unproductive scrubland now supports orchards, vineyards, and melon cultivation. The level surface and low population density make the area suitable for airforce installations. Finally, the coastal façade of the Crau is the setting of the most spectacular change, the port and industrial complex of Fos-sur-Mer.

Between the two main branches of the Rhône lies the Camargue, a flat area of lagoon and marsh which until recent times was one of the most mysterious and romantic areas of France. The centre of the Camargue, now protected as a nature reserve and regional park, preserves its natural character and is a haven for wildlife and the traditional, but much diminished, economy of wild bull and horse rearing. The Camargue is an environmental battlefield where fresh water meets salt water, and variations in land-use

The port and agglomeration of Marseille

Port Autonome de Marseille

correspond with hydrological conditions. Distributed as an arc around three sides of the central zone, the agricultural Camargue consists of reclaimed land, given over to vines, fruit, and above all, rice-growing. The last-named, centred on Arles, is in slight regression but still supplies the great majority of French internal consumption.

The Marseille–Aix–Berre complex

It would be difficult to find a more striking contrast in the whole of the Lower Rhône region than that between the delta zone, with its extremely low population density and absence of relief barriers, and the area immediately to the east, with its confining mountain chains but highest population concentrations and highest levels of economic activity in the whole of the French Midi. The physical background is of alternating limestone ranges and semi-enclosed basins, producing a fragmentation in the distribution of resources and a compartmentalization of economic and social activity. Problems of co-ordination of development are posed in an area that is by nature disjointed. At the heart of the zone's economy is the Marseille agglomeration of over a million inhabitants, France's leading seaport and an important industrial city. Constrained by the Estaque, Etoile, and Saint-Cyr ranges, Marseille has turned westwards to the Etang de Berre to accommodate its port and industrial expansion and to locate its overspill population. The Etang de Berre, with over 200 000 inhabitants around its shores, is essentially an annexe to Marseille, initiated by the need to accommodate ever-larger ships and now developing as an important industrial zone in its own right. The springboard for industrial development was petroleum refining and the petrochemical industry, but increasingly metallurgical, engineering, and light industries employ large numbers. The launching of the Fos-sur-Mer project has confirmed the westward movement in the economic centre of gravity of the Marseille urbanized area and calls into question the future of the Etang de Berre annexe and the nature of its integration with the city of Marseille.

To the north of Marseille, the basins of Aix-en-Provence and Gardanne are also the settings of urban development. Aix is now linked to Marseille by motorway, its university, cultural, residential, and administrative functions complementing the industrial and commercial functions of that city. The Gardanne basin is primarily agricultural, but the lignite field supplies power to a major alumina plant.

The Lower Durance valley

To the north of the Chaîne des Côtes, the Durance valley below Cadarache has a double orientation. The lower portion, centred on Cavaillon, is virtually an annexe to the Comtat Venaissin; but most of the Lower Durance, by virtue of the harnessing of the river for hydro-electricity, municipal water supply, and irrigation, is linked with the Marseille agglomeration and its environs. It is perhaps the best example in France of a formerly unstable environment, plagued by both floods and excessively low water levels, that has been successfully harnessed by means of multi-purpose water control for the benefit of man.

Nîmes and the Costières du Gard

To the west of the delta, a rapid transition takes place in the direction of another major geographical region, the plain of Bas-Languedoc. The eastern portion of this plain, consisting of a low-lying littoral backed by the more elevated Costières du Gard dominated by Nîmes, has strong connections with the Lower Rhône region in terms both of communications and of economic orientation. Nîmes is an ancient city currently undergoing rapid expansion, expressed in massive apartment complexes and commercial centres on the periphery of the agglomeration. The predominance of vines on the lowland reminds one that this is a zone transitional to France's largest wine-producing area, Bas-Languedoc. However, the diversion of water from the Rhône is permitting diversification into farming activities more typical of Provence and the Rhône valley than of Languedoc. On the coast the new tourist complexes of La Grande Motte and Port Camargue represent an extension of the planned tourist expansion of the Languedoc coast to the margins of the Rhône delta.

In varying degrees, each of the five components described has undergone transformation since World War II. Although some of the problems have been shared, notably in the sphere of water control, each sub-region has encountered its own difficulties of adjustment and, in spite of the progress made, retains distinctive problems at the present time.

2 Problems of Social and Economic Development

Perhaps the fascination of the Lower Rhône region to the geographer is the manner in which new problems have arisen as old ones have been solved. The landscape bears eloquent testimony to the perennial struggle against an environment that is rich in promise but uncompromising in its requirement of a rational and integrated approach to resource use. The mosaic of windbreaks in the Comtat Venaissin and the network of irrigation canals on the Durance plain testify to the fact that the abundant potential of the region can be exploited only by a close adjustment of techniques to an environment which can be bountiful and vindictive in turn. Whereas the struggle to maintain environmental stability may be traced back to antiquity, the spectre of pollution and traffic congestion has raised its head only relatively recently. Some problems, like those of urban renewal and port development at Marseille, are a product of man-made organizations rather than of the natural environment.

The Lower Rhône is a region where technology has been invoked on a massive scale as an answer to both environmental and human problems. Indeed, in some instances, the use of applied technology has outpaced the capacity of administration, planning, and decision-making to achieve the maximum advantage in human and social terms of the new opportunities thus offered. In turn this has given birth to a new problem with many facets, that of achieving the optimum organization of space so as to maximize economic efficiency, whilst preserving congenial living, working, and recreational conditions. The present chapter seeks to identify and explain the range of problems that have faced the region since World War II. The treatment is inevitably summary since the range of problems is wide and their individual complexity great. Further detail, however, is added in the third section of this book which analyses the planned attack on the region's problems.

Four broad categories of problem may be proposed as characterizing all or part of the Lower Rhône region: the quest for environmental stability, the need to exploit underutilized resources, the specific problems of the Marseille agglomeration, and the search for a balanced and integrated organization of space.

The quest for environmental stability

The highly individual nature of the Mediterranean environment is the essential backcloth to all human endeavour in the region. To the

The quest for environmental stability: windbreaks and irrigation canals in the Lower Durance valley   I.N.R.A.

difficulties of the classic Mediterranean climatic régime of prolonged dry spells and excessive summer heat are added the vagaries of powerful rivers nourished by mountain climates outside the region, the icy mistral wind, and the ever-present risk of devastating fires. The environment in effect imposes a state of siege on man's use of resources, in which production without protection and conservation is hazardous. The landscape is thus largely artificial, reflecting the effort of man to safeguard against flood, fire, wind, rain, heat, and cold, in order to gain the rich rewards bestowed by a long growing season.

The key to successful production is water control. During the long summer, and even into autumn, the comparatively few rain days coupled with intense moisture loss by rapid infiltration and evapotranspiration, impoverish the crop range, reduce yields, and retard growth unless irrigation is practised. The trilogy of cereals, olives, and vines, dry-farmed in areas lacking irrigation, was the standard response throughout Mediterranean France but offers no basis for a modern competitive agricultural economy. Water control, involving the storage and distribution of water throughout entire drainage basins, in turn permitting flood control, is the prime factor in the mastery of the environment. In spite of the irregular and often erratic nature of the rainfall régime, the region is in fact rich in water resources. The Durance and Verdon are essentially mountain rivers, nourished by the Alpine rainfall and snow melt and possessing a huge total annual discharge, but one subject to seasonal variation. The use of their precious water is thus dependent on storage capacity in order to regulate their flow, avoid disastrous flooding, and regularize the capricious channel of the lower Durance. The Rhône, fed by both the Alps and the Massif Central is a virtually inexhaustible water supply, but the size and power of the river poses enormous problems of control, soluble only by technology and civil engineering of a high order. If the total water budget available to the region is more than adequate to offset the deficiencies of the precipitation régime, its control and distribution nevertheless pose difficulties and expense that were beyond the expertise and financial capacity of previous generations of farmers. Large areas of the Lower Rhône region, and especially the basins to the north and east of Marseille, drained only by short rivers and ephemeral streams and separated by relief barriers from the major rivers, have only recently acquired access to irrigation water, and the process is even now not completed. In the historical past, the problem of water distribution was partially solved by an elaborate network of feeder canals, but storage and long-distance distribution is a comparatively recent feature and, significantly, has been coupled with hydro-electricity development. The immediate economic return in the form of energy facilitates the longer term investment in agricultural improvement.

Although water control is the key to environmental stability and increased output, it is by no means the only strategy. Indeed in some ways it is the most straightforward task in that solutions applied in one locality can be adapted to others, the basic technology being transferable and the main constraint being that of cost. Extremes of temperature, wind, and storms pose severe problems at specific seasons. The advantages of high temperatures and insolation are partially offset by the damage caused by sudden frosts in spring and autumn, the more so as these affect high-value crops accounting for a high proportion of the cash income to individual farms. Similarly, torrential storms in late summer and early autumn coincide with the critical harvest period in the vineyards. Protection against both these hazards can be only partial. By contrast, every effort is made to combat the additional scourge of the mistral. This north wind, sucking in freezing air from the Alps and Massif Central, can assume great violence, exceeding 100 kilometres per hour at Avignon and on the delta, and can blow continuously for as long as ten days. Protection against the violence is achieved by hedgerows of cypress, poplars, and live and dead canes, aligned against the wind. Protection against this wind, which can level crops and strip trees, is incomplete however, the pattern of hedgerows itself generating eddies and counter-currents, and research is currently being undertaken into the most effective alignment pattern for windbreaks.

The direct effects of climate, in terms of hydrological conditions and weather extremes, pose the principal threat to environmental stability, but indirect effects are also significant. First amongst these is the character of the vegetation formed under Mediterranean climatic conditions. The natural climax vegetation has been virtually eliminated from the lowlands and plateaux giving way to *maquis* woodland and *garrigue* scrub over much of the non-agricultural land. This degraded vegetation has correspondingly little economic value as a direct resource for use as timber or grazing. It does, however, form an attractive setting for recreation, for camp sites, and for rural 'second homes'. Allied to the limited economic value is its combustibility under summer conditions of extreme dryness, so that whether induced by natural phenomena, such as lightning, or more commonly by human carelessness, fires are an endemic threat. When there are strong winds, fires spread at great speed, destroying in their path homes and more valuable forest resources. In the Lower Rhône region, the *maquis* and forest cover is restricted primarily to the surrounding uplands and the destruction is principally to amenity rather than to productive timber capacity, but amenity is fast becoming a valued resource.

A further problem attributable to the climate is the paucity of natural grasses. Except where irrigation is practised, as on the Crau, the natural grasses yield poor pasture. Even sheep, formerly reared in large numbers on the Crau, had to be taken to Alpine pastures during the desiccating summer. The region is deficient in animal produce, yet in its natural condition can support only extensive grazing, principally on the peripheral plateaux, beyond the reach of irrigation and thus of possible intensification.

Soil conditions are highly variable, in composition, depth, and fertility. Much of the upland karst has shallow rendzina soils and even the lowlands are commonly composed of extensive tracts of coarse detrital material. The range of soil types, from deep but saline soils in parts of the Camargue to virtual pavements of pebbles in the Crau, seems infinite and furthermore, over much of the region, drainage, irrigation, and fertilization have left few of the soils in a natural condition. Even fertility is not necessarily a sure guide to productive worth, for valuable olive groves and vineyards grow in a rubble soil on the flanks of the upland chains and on the Comtat Venaissin, the insolation being reflected by the white pebbles and the vines yielding wine with a high alcohol content. For many crops (especially vines and delicate fruit trees) aspect, drainage conditions, and microclimate count as much as soil conditions. Nevertheless, while soil conditions impose few insuperable barriers to successful farming throughout most of the region, they do dictate particular choices of crop combination.

The quest for environmental stability is basic to an understanding of the landscape of the Lower Rhône region, and indeed the whole of Lower Provence. The astonishing opulence and variety of farm produce in the area is testament to an endeavour, spread over many centuries, to achieve a control over difficult but rewarding natural conditions. Even so, the nature of this control has been revolutionized since World War II, primarily by more effective water control, and innovations have appeared that have transformed the landscape. To the vines, soft fruits, and early vegetables have been added hundreds of hectares of rice fields and irrigated apple orchards. Rough grazing has been transformed into irrigated pasture and fruit farms. As later discussion will show, the problem of controlling the environment has in large measure been solved at the cost of massive investment but it would be too much to claim that the environment has been completely stabilized. Irrigation works alter the delicate hydrological balance. The discharge of the diverted Durance into the Etang de Berre has eliminated the marine fish and populated it with eels. Atmospheric and water pollution have accompanied industrial development and the *maquis*, a valuable amenity and wildlife habitat, has retreated before the tide of development. The nature of the environmental problem is therefore changing from one of control, based on healthy respect born of experience, to one of misuse by an increasingly urban industrial society possessing values radically different from those of previous generations of agriculturalists.

Under-utilization of resources

At the close of World War II, the Lower Rhône region, in common with most of the French Midi, was an under-developed region. Apart from Marseille, no town exceeded 50 000 inhabitants and the economy was overwhelmingly rural. The region's main assets—abundant water for irrigation and electricity generation, the Rhône routeway, and climatic conditions favouring both an intensification of commercial farming and an expansion of tourism—lay untapped. In effect, the region suffered from an under-utilization of its resources, limiting the possibilities of economic and social development and leading to a stagnation in urban growth and a drift of population from the less-favoured rural areas. This under-utilization stemmed in part from the environmental constraints outlined above and in part from human inertia brought about by a lack of investment, persistence of traditional methods and attitudes, and deficiencies of the transport infrastructure. Marseille apart, the region was characterized by small-scale operation, whether in the agricultural economy or in industry, and by lack of a driving force. A further characteristic, therefore, was the tendency for fragmentation of economic and social organization, each *pays* having its particular economic emphasis and each town a related specialization. This is not to say that the region was poor, for climatic conditions guaranteed a range of early-season crops which gave it a competitive edge over other regions and a ready market in northern France for its produce. Nevertheless, the region failed to exploit available and potential resources, and in particular was under-industrialized.

In the more leisurely atmosphere of the inter-war years, when farmers' livelihoods were protected by the powerful agricultural lobby in parliament, when artisan-scale industry still seemed secure, and when Marseille prospered on a captive colonial trade, the under-exploitation of resources scarcely seemed a pressing problem. Indeed, the grace and charm of the towns, the opulence of the agricultural landscape, the thriving trade of Marseille, and the lethargy imposed by the summer heat conspired to give the region a sense of timelessness, as one of the most distinctive and eternal regions of France. Moreover, under-industrialization was not restricted to the Lower Rhône, for virtually all but Paris and the north-east quadrant of France was predominantly agricultural as late as 1940.

The circumstances of the post-war period placed an entirely different perspective on resource use. To sustain the nation's spectacular economic and demographic revival, every region was required to produce more and to do so more efficiently. By the 1950s France had embarked on an ambitious programme of modernization, blueprinted in the successive national plans, which called into question workshop scale and methods of production and haphazard marketing systems, and required manpower to be moved from an overloaded rural sector to more productive occupations sited in the expanding towns. This programme gained impetus from the advent in the late 1950s of regional planning, and from the competitive stimulus provided by the Common Market. The modernization of the Lower Rhône region became a national priority as a factor helping to redress the maldistribution of industry in France and because the under-use of resources, both material and human, represented a wastage that the country could not afford in its effort to raise output and living standards.

The most under-used resource, as indicated above, was water. This was the more serious since it represented the wastage of a multi-purpose resource, capable of raising agricultural output, improving navigation, supplying the needs of industry, and bringing energy to an area deficient in indigenous fuel sources other than the Gardanne lignite field. The problems inherent in harnessing rivers as powerful as the

Rhône and the Durance were enormous, both in technical and cost terms; but given a national situation of inadequate and increasingly uneconomic coal reserves, mounting imports of petroleum, and a rapid exhaustion of the available mountain sites for hydro-electricity generation, these rivers represented a national as well as a regional priority. In fact, the harnessing of the Durance was completed before that of the Rhône, work on the more productive upper and middle sections of the Rhône valley—outside the region—being completed before attention was turned to the lower section.

The exploitation of the Rhône routeway has also been a national priority since World War II, but with different strategies applied to the different modes of transport. Before the war, the Rhône corridor below Lyon performed primarily a transit function serving the port of Marseille, carrying tourist traffic bound for the Riviera, and moving agricultural produce. Transport of industrial goods on an international scale tended to be diverted over the Alpine passes, and the Rhône route provided only a weak stimulus to industrialization below Lyon. In its unimproved state the waterway itself had little significance internally and virtually none internationally.

The modernization of the railway system has proved a relatively straightforward task, the process of electrification naturally accompanying that of the early hydro-electricity development. Equally significant, however, has been the construction of *marché-gares* with specialized sidings, speeding the transfer of perishable farm produce and streamlining marketing procedures. Similarly, the bulk transfer of crude and refined petroleum along the Rhône route by pipeline posed few technical difficulties. The establishment of a motorway link from Marseille to Paris via Lyon was a national priority which has enhanced the Rhône route and the Lower Rhône in particular. The extensions of this motorway spine into Languedoc and towards Nice make the Lower Rhône region a natural focal point.

The final element in the pattern of movement is the Rhône itself, but improvement to the waterway has lagged behind improvements to other modes of transport. Two problems hinder an increased use of the river. Continuous high capacity will not be achieved until all the power schemes between Lyon and the delta have been completed, and the link to the Rhine is still non-existent and denies the waterway a sufficient penetration to a highly industrialized hinterland. The creation of Fos makes the improvement of navigation all the more crucial. However, the further exploitation of the Rhône corridor is basically a question of time and money. A more fundamental question remains. Will the Lower Rhône remain simply a more efficient artery of transit and communication, or will it become a true axis of growth, with frequent industrial concentrations along its length?

The problem of expanding and intensifying agricultural output has become an economic and organizational problem rather than an environmental one. The key environmental problem, that of assuring a supply of irrigation water and protection from inundation, has been largely solved by the control of the Rhône and Durance. Dry-farmed areas have been converted to intensive production and new specializations have been introduced. As a result of the vastly increased area under intensive cultivation, together with improvement in the quality of traditional commodities such as wine, problems of over-production have now appeared. Basically, the Lower Rhône now produces commodities dependent on an expanding demand from affluent markets. Considerable effort has gone into the perfection of quality, maximization of yields, careful calibration, and packaging of produce. The end result is an expensive product difficult to market in the quantities produced. The problem has been aggravated by the failure of the region's processing industries to expand at a rate capable of absorbing the surplus production. With an ever-increasing area being put under orchards, the problem of marketing is fraught with uncertainty which co-operative organization and more efficient wholesale structures can only partially offset. The region is vulnerable to consumer reaction against high prices, exacerbated during periods of recession or inflation within the European market.

Another under-used material resource is one of tourist amenities. The Lower Rhône region has a magnificent endowment of natural features and man-made monuments to attract both holidaymakers and *en passant* tourists heading for other regions. In the past, the *en passant* element has tended to dominate, attracted by cultural centres such as Avignon and Aix, or by ancient monuments such as the Pont du Gard meriting a detour. The scale of development does not match that of the Côte d'Azur or the Alps, and the Lower Rhône lacks the mass tourism that brings employment and a high revenue. In particular, the coast west of the Camargue was virtually one of virgin beaches until recently. It could be argued with force that to have escaped

mass tourism is a matter for congratulation, but to some extent this is misleading. Apart from the economic loss, the resultant pattern tends to be one of *ad hoc* development, of badly sited camping sites, uncontrolled parking, and an expansion of second homes into areas warranting complete protection. The problem, therefore, is to gain greater economic return from an increased volume of tourism, expanding facilities while protecting the amenity value of the landscape.

The final resource, under-used in the past is not material but human. Before World War II, agricultural occupations dominated employment, followed by service occupations, with manufacturing a poor third and of major significance in only a limited number of localities. The labour force was concentrated into sectors with relatively low productivity and with only modest growth potential as far as employment opportunities were concerned. The region was deficient in two main types of employment: work for women and suitable employment for the better qualified post-war generation of school- and university-leavers. Work was also needed for labour released from agriculture following its increased mechanization, the heavy demand during harvest periods being met by casual labourers who included a high proportion of immigrants. The low female activity rate, the post-war demographic revival with its unprecedented growth in the number of young people entering the labour market, and the general raising of both educational qualifications and job expectations increased the need for economic expansion if human resources were not to be under-used or entirely lost to the region by migration.

Given the persistent decline of full-time employment in agriculture and the fact that commercial activity was already well developed, the prime need was for industrial employment. Industrial growth was necessary both for its direct and its induced effects. Only industrial growth could provide the volume and range of remunerative employment required, but in addition, the growth of manufacturing was needed to stimulate employment in the service sector, to promote port activity, and to generate employment in building and public works. Industrialization called for new roads, port extension, increased energy production and transmission, the creation of industrial estates, and thus new employment in construction activities including qualified labour. The process of industrialization also required an expansion and reorientation of educational facilities. In particular the scientific and technical branches of higher education needed to be reinforced, and research facilities expanded, so that the region's universities could both nourish and support industrial growth. Finally, industrialization required an increased mobility of labour, both geographically, from the villages and smaller towns to new industrial growth centres, and by sector, from agricultural and artisan activities to manufacturing. In turn this increased the need for new transport systems, programmes of housing construction in the reception areas, and improvements in the dissemination of information concerning employment opportunities.

Problems of the Marseille agglomeration

By virtue of its size, complexity, and special functions, the problems of Marseille are distinctive and worthy of separate consideration. Throughout its modern history Marseille has occupied a special place in the economic geography of France. Its rise to prominence as the nation's largest port owed more to its situation than to any inherent site advantage of its entirely artificial port. Marseille was admirably placed to gather the colonial trade of North Africa, the trade currents of the Mediterranean basin and the Middle East, and, via the Suez Canal, the Far Eastern colonial trade. In turn, the transit of raw commodities fostered the growth of processing industries, breaking down bulk materials into semi-finished products for onward transmission within France. Accordingly, Marseille developed vegetable-oil refining, sugar and cocoa processing, and related food and chemical industries, together with ancillary port activities such as building and repairing ships. Both trade and industry stimulated commercial activity, and between the wars Marseille was firmly established as a thriving port city of half a million inhabitants. It was, however, essentially a national port, monopolizing the colonial passenger and cargo traffic for the whole of France. Marseille did not benefit from a regional hinterland of any strength,

Port and industrial expansion to the west of Marseille: the petroleum port and B.P. refinery at Lavéra; in the background, Port-de-Bouc and the Caronte basin
Port Autonome de Marseille

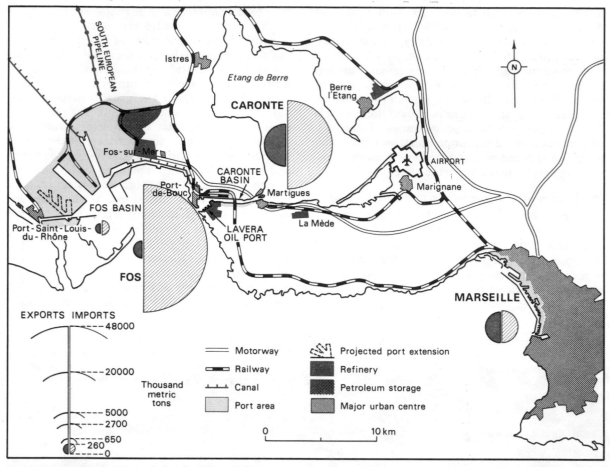

Fig. 2 The Marseille—Etang de Berre port complex

nor did it, in turn, greatly stimulate the regional economy. The smaller ports of the Mediterranean—Sète, Port-la-Nouvelle, Port-Saint-Louis-du-Rhône—established local hinterlands in the Midi for their trade in agricultural exports and specialized imports. Even before World War II, a significant trend had emerged with the establishment of the specialized oil port at Lavéra on the Etang de Berre, at a site capable of accepting the largest tankers then in existence and, unlike Marseille, possessing open space for the related industries, refining and petrochemicals, to expand.

The post-war history of Marseille is a fascinating study in adjustment which is still evolving. The port has had to adjust to a number of fundamental changes beyond its power to control. The advent of mass air transport has robbed Marseille of a vital element in its traditional traffic, the long-distance passenger liner. The same phenomenon has, nevertheless, produced a major international airport which is

now one of the city's main assets. Much more significant, since it hit the port's basic trade, was the loss of the North African colonies, especially Algeria, and the closure of the Suez Canal, blocking off Far Eastern routes. At the same time, ships have grown in size to a stage exceeding the navigational limits and handling facilities of the original port. The port has made its adjustment in two ways, structurally and geographically. Structural changes have been made in the composition of traffic, the decline in liner traffic being partially offset by the growth of shorter-distance car ferry traffic and cruising, and the stagnation in general cargo handling being more than compensated for by a spectacular increase in bulk cargo, especially petroleum. This latter trend accounts for the progressive geographical shift westwards in the port's activity, at least as far as cargo handling is concerned. The ever-increasing size of petroleum tankers, and latterly of mineral carriers, has resulted in a demand for deep-water terminals with adjacent vacant land for storage, processing, and distribution, initially found at the entrance to the Etang de Berre and more recently at the Gulf of Fos.

This structural and geographical shift has brought both benefits and problems. On the one hand, the dramatic rise in petroleum imports has enabled Marseille to expand enormously the volume of tonnage handled in spite of the relative decline of traditional traffic. The development of specialized annexes has also eased the congestion of the initial port, hemmed in as it is by a dense agglomeration on all sides. On the other hand, the decline of general cargo at Marseille, coupled with increased mechanization, roll-on/roll-off facilities and container handling, has meant a drastic reduction in employment in the docks. Furthermore, the growth of petroleum traffic results in an enormous disparity between imports and exports. Whereas the trade of Marseille itself is well balanced, that of the annexes is heavily distorted in favour of imports (Fig. 2). Finally, the fragmentation of the port complex administered by Marseille, which includes the Caronte Basin, Fos, and Port-Saint-Louis-du-Rhône, makes for problems of organization and co-ordination. In theory the various elements of the port complement each other rather than compete, as far as the type of trade is concerned. Nevertheless, there is an element of rivalry in terms of investment and the creation of employment which complicates decision-making, not only for the port authority but in the wider planning field. The decision to expand one element rather than another inevitably affects the planning of transport, the location of industry, and the provision of housing and services. The decision to build the Fos port/industrial complex, for example, has led to a complete reorientation of future growth in the Marseille metropolitan area.

In addition to the problems of the port, Marseille experiences other difficulties more severe in scale than elsewhere in the Lower Rhône region. Chief of these is the problem of physical expansion as a consequence of rapid population growth. Between 1954 and 1962 the Marseille agglomeration increased its population by almost 18 per cent, and between 1962 and 1968 by almost 15 per cent. This represents an annual average increase of up to 20 000 inhabitants of which three-quarters have been accounted for by migrants, and therefore by persons in search of housing and employment. Given the congested building pattern of the central agglomeration, this population expansion has resulted in suburban extension. The physical growth of the built-up area has, however, been constrained by the accidented relief, necessitating high-density apartment development on available sites. In turn this poses the problem of providing adequate services for the new and populous residential satellites, which generate large currents of commuters, straining public transport, road, and parking facilities.

The problem of housing the additional population is complicated by the need for urban renewal in the heart of the agglomeration. This is a problem of many facets. It involves the rehousing of the population at present occupying decayed buildings, as has been attempted for example around the Vieux Port. There is also a question of rehousing the population excluded as a result of former residential areas being infiltrated by business activities, whether spontaneously on the margin of the central business district, or, as is increasingly the case, by planned city-centre redevelopment. Finally there is a social problem, in that urban renewal in the city centre involves an attack on areas habitually harbouring crime and vice or sheltering poorly-assimilated immigrant groups. As a great international port, Marseille has long been France's most cosmopolitan provincial city, and the existence of a criminal underworld has been a recognized feature of the city. More recently, a second social problem, that of racial tension, has become significant. The large North African population, employed primarily in the construction industry, is poorly assimilated, and the return of French repatriates from Algeria has added to the growth of prejudice against the native North Africans.

The problem of traffic congestion is more acute in Marseille than elsewhere in the region. This stems from the high concentration of activity and employment at the heart of the agglomeration—the central business district and port being juxtaposed—and also from different forms of traffic using the same roads. The conflict between heavy port traffic, commuter movement, the commercial activity of the business district, and inter-urban traffic, inevitably produces congestion which even the construction of new intra-urban motorways has not resolved at peak hours.

A further problem of Marseille concerns its industrial base. In relation to the importance of its port, Marseille has never been heavily industrialized. Employment has been in the processing sector, notably foodstuffs, rather than in manufacturing activities involving advanced technology, high added value, and rapid growth rates.

A new elevated motorway under construction in Marseille to relieve traffic congestion in the port zone

These last-named types of industry have characterized the new port annexes and the airport zone, distant from the main concentration of population. Moreoever, post-war expansion around the Etang de Berre has tended to be capital-intensive, in refining and petrochemicals for example, rather than in industries employing large numbers of workers. In the case of petroleum, much of the crude oil merely moves through the terminals via pipelines to distant inland refineries. The city of Marseille lacks substantial, expanding, and interlinked manufacturing companies, capable of providing a growing and varied range of employment. It suffers a relatively high unemployment rate and a low female activity rate, and is lacking in the well-qualified occupations.

A final problem is that of co-ordinated future development, not merely in the existing agglomeration, but throughout its metropolitan region. The difficulties of the site coupled with the fragmentation of the port and the tendency for new industry to move to locations away from the city, sited on industrial estates close to motor-ways or near the port annexes, have produced a new and looser pattern of development, spanning numerous administrative authorities and posing serious difficulties for long-term planning. This particular problem raises the need to achieve a rational and coherent organization of space, not only to solve existing problems but as a framework for strategic planning throughout the Marseille city region.

The future organization of space

The need to achieve such a functional organization of space, which on the one hand promotes economic efficiency, and on the other makes for a rational use of human and physical resources while maintaining the quality of the environment, is a problem affecting not only Marseille, but the whole of the Lower Rhône region. Clearly a coherent administrative framework, a harmonious urban hierarchy, a balanced distribution of economic activity, an even distribution of population, a highly articulated transport network and a co-ordinated approach to planning decisions confer enormous benefits in terms of the

The latest trend in industrial location: the new industrial estate at Vitrolles served by the A7 motorway

quality of life. That such a spatial organization has not yet been achieved in the Lower Rhône region is a problem with many causes.

In part the problem results from the breakdown of existing sub-regional specializations with their simple town–country relationships, as exemplified by the traditional agricultural zones with their market towns. The innovations in transport, the expansion of industry, and the demographic and urban explosions have all reacted on the old, rather circumscribed patterns of pre-war life. Inevitably, certain sub-regions and towns have progressed whilst others have lost ground. Certain rural areas, hitherto stagnating demographically, are now overwhelmed by suburban expansion, tourist development, or the infiltration of second homes. Such a trend when spread over a long time may pose no difficulty, and a natural adjustment occurs spontaneously. When these changes are compressed into a very short period, and when (as in the Lower Rhône region) they give every indication of further rapid evolution, the problems are more acute.

It may be suggested that the future organiza-

tion of the Lower Rhône region should be one that is integrated within itself whilst at the same time being compatible with development in adjacent regions. The Lower Rhône enjoys certain advantages in the search for this ideal but also suffers some difficulties. External co-ordination is favoured by the existence of major development schemes which traverse regional boundaries, as in the Rhône and Durance valleys and on the Languedoc plain. Such schemes ensure an integrated use of resources and mutual benefits. Similarly, improved lines of communication by rail and motorway ensure that there are no physical obstacles to co-ordinated development either internally or externally. On the other hand, the Lower Rhône does not have a perfectly adjusted urban network and hierarchy. Fig. 3 demonstrates the uneven character of the network and the variation in contemporary growth rates. It is clear that in general the smaller towns are experiencing the highest growth rates, especially by migration, whereas the larger urban centres, which continue to dominate in the provision of higher order services, have expanded more slowly. Smaller

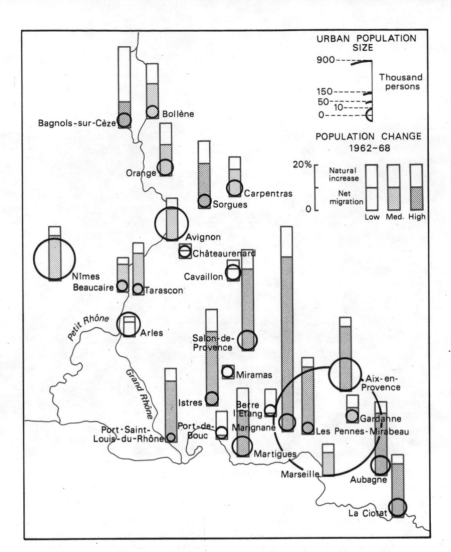

Fig. 3   The urban network

URBAN POPULATION
SIZE

900----

150----
50----
10----
0----

Thousand
persons

POPULATION CHANGE
1962-68

20% Natural
increase

Net
migration
0

Low Med. High

Bagnols-sur-Cèze
Bollène
Orange
Carpentras
Sorgues
Avignon
Châteaurenard
Cavaillon
Nîmes
Beaucaire
Tarascon
Petit Rhône
Arles
Salon-de-Provence
Grand Rhône
Miramas
Aix-en-Provence
Istres
Berre l'Etang
Gardanne
Port-Saint-Louis-du-Rhône
Port-de-Bouc
Marignane
Les Pennes-Mirabeau
Martigues
Marseille
Aubagne
La Ciotat

towns to the north and west, in particular, are under pressure and are likely to grow even more in the future, given the trends in industrial location. At the head of the urban hierarchy, Marseille is not a completely effective regional capital in spite of its size. It does not animate or exercise full control over the regional economy. One of the effects of the development of the Etang de Berre—Fos complex, for example, has been to introduce national and international firms directed from head offices outside the region. Nor is Marseille at the head of a unified administrative and planning organization for the whole of the Lower Rhône region. The area, as already observed, is divided between three *départements* and is formed of parts of two planning regions. This fragmentation of administration inevitably interposes an obstacle to a more rational organization of space.

The previous chapter attempted to identify the broad categories of problem present in the Lower Rhône region. They were characterized as varying in nature, changing with the passage of time, and, in some instances, extending beyond the confines of the area under consideration. These problems have not been passively accepted, but rather the Lower Rhône region has become a virtual test bed of planned regional development in the post-war period. The present chapter seeks to describe the progress made towards solutions through the agency of the various development plans and projects. In some instances the planning organization is Government con-

trolled, whereas in others a local government structure is involved. In several instances a blending of both public and private sectors forms the basis of a mixed economy organization. Above all, this approach demonstrates that French regional planning is not a uniform monolithic structure, but a range of plans, policies, and strategies, with the precise organizational structure being adjusted to the scale and character of the individual development problems. Six examples of planned development are discussed, which in total involve virtually the whole of the Lower Rhône region. In several instances, the scope of development extends well beyond the region,

Fig. 4   The development of the Rhône by the C.N.R.; (inset) projects in the Lower Rhône

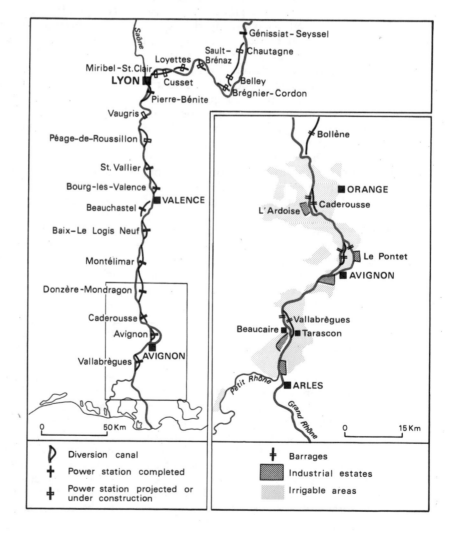

and in these cases the entire project will be summarized briefly before considering in greater detail its impact within the Lower Rhône region. The first three such projects have in common the controlled use of water resources.

Development of the Rhône

Pride of place in any discussion of development in the Lower Rhône region must be accorded to the work undertaken by the Compagnie Nationale du Rhône (C.N.R.) because of the scale of its effort, the multi-purpose nature of its objectives, and its potential European significance. The activities of the C.N.R. illustrate very well the shift away from limited objectives to a comprehensive view of planned development. Control and development of the Rhône is in fact a key element in several other schemes considered below, notably the construction of Fos-sur-Mer and irrigation in Bas-Languedoc.

The C.N.R. was created in 1931 by the combined interests of local authorities, the Paris–Lyon–Méditerranée railway company, the *département* of Seine, and electricity companies and consumers in the Paris and Lyon regions, under overall Government supervision. With the subsequent nationalization of the railways and the creation of a State electricity company, which greatly increased public investment, the State is now the dominant partner, but the mixed economy structure remains. The company was founded to realize three objectives: (1) the harnessing of energy by the construction of twenty power schemes between the Swiss frontier and the sea, providing electricity for industrial and domestic use and for the railway, (2) the control of the river's erratic flow so as to reduce flooding and extend irrigation, and (3) the improvement of navigation. Hampered by the war, the company made a slow start and investment was concentrated initially where returns would be most quickly realized, in the sphere of hydro-electricity generation. Attention was naturally focused on the sites with the greatest production potential, in the mountain tract above Lyon, and the Génissiat and Seyssel schemes were completed between 1949 and 1951 (Fig. 4).

Given this initial investment and the continuation of energy shortages after the war, priority continued to be given to hydro-electricity throughout the 1950s and into the 1960s. Investment was concentrated still on sites yielding the highest return, in practice the basins and defiles of the Middle Rhône between Lyon and Donzère, where the steepest natural gradients occur. In contrast with the mountain sites, the existence of densely populated and fertile lowland have prohibited reservoir construction and necessitated instead the building of barrages and long diversion canals to accumulate a head of water at the power stations, which are in turn by-passed by navigation locks. The Donzère-Mondragon scheme, completed in 1952, marked a significant turning point, for in addition to electricity generation the scheme involved the construction of a new waterway and the irrigation of the adjacent lowland. The success of Donzère-Mondragon paved the way for five similar schemes in the Middle Rhône valley by 1971, leaving two further schemes, at Vaugris and Péage-de-Roussillon, to be built before 1978 to complete the equipment of this section of the valley.

Meanwhile, the early 1960s had brought a change in emphasis in the company's policy, thus far concerned primarily with energy production. In 1962 the Pierre-Bénite scheme was begun on the southern fringe of Lyon. Although this yielded only modest amounts of electricity, the construction of the barrage permitted the creation of a new industrial estate at Feyzin, and the junction of the Rhône and Saône navigational systems. The activities of the C.N.R. thus moved into the wider sphere of economic development, a trend subsequently reinforced in the 1960s by the decision to extend activities beyond the Middle Rhône to the Lower Rhône region and, above Lyon, to the Saône valley. The decision to extend improvements to other sections before the completion of the Middle Rhône tract stemmed from several considerations of which the need to improve the Rhône–Saône waterway was the key element. The barrages of the Middle Rhône, whilst improving navigation, did so along only a limited section of the river, leaving Lyon still unconnected by deep waterway with the Lower Rhône and Marseille. The decision to build the new port/industrial complex at Fos-sur-Mer, close to the mouth of the Rhône, gave the matter new urgency. The success of the Fos operation depends on the creation of a large and accessible hinterland. Conversely, the function of Fos as the seaport for the powerful and expanding Lyon industrial region depends in part on the establishment of an effective waterway connection. In the longer term, the Rhône is destined to form part of a trans-European link joining the Rhine and Danube to the Rhône, with Rotterdam and Fos–Marseille as the two terminal poles. The nature and timing of this link are as yet unspecified, but a route via the Doubs valley to Alsace has priority and could be completed in the early 1980s.

Improvement of the Rhône by the C.N.R. at Avignon. The view, looking south, shows the two power stations permitted by the branching of the river and, in the centre, the navigation canal

25

Activities of the C.N.R. in the Lower Rhône region

The decision to carry out the integrated development of the Rhône has brought the activities of the C.N.R. firmly into the Lower Rhône region, previously affected only by the Donzère-Mondragon scheme. Fig. 4 indicates that the multi-purpose nature of the C.N.R.'s role has been maintained and even strengthened.

The improvement of the Lower Rhône valley below Donzère has several aspects. Three barrages with power stations and navigation locks are involved above Tarascon–Beaucaire—at Caderousse, Avignon, and Vallabrègues—whilst south of Tarascon, the Grand Rhône is being dredged to complete a deep water link to Port-Saint-Louis and the Fos complex, and the Petit Rhône improved to establish a waterway link with the Canal du Rhône à Sète. The construction of power stations is particularly difficult, for although the fall of the river is at a minimum, the force is at a maximum. The output of the three power schemes will not be enormous, but it will be sufficient to meet the present energy needs of the entire Marseille agglomeration. The Vallabrègues scheme was commissioned in 1970, and in addition to protecting large areas of productive agricultural land from flooding it has enabled the establishment of a port and industrial zone on previously flood-prone land at Courtine, at the confluence with the Durance. The Avignon scheme occupies a natural branching of the river which has been considerably modified. The branching of the river has permitted the construction of two power stations, whilst the straightening of the western branch has improved navigation and created an artificial island to be developed for recreational use. The scheme, completed in 1973, has given increased flood protection to Avignon and its industrial suburb of Le Pontet, as well as to the low-lying agricultural land of the Ile de la Barthelasse. The Caderousse scheme, currently under construction and scheduled for completion in 1975, will give flood protection to the town of Caderousse and the surrounding agricultural plain, and will bring improved canal access to the port and industrial complex of l'Ardoise.

Below Tarascon, the effort is primarily one of dredging, with the multiple purpose of increasing the head of water at the Vallabrègues power station, opening the Grand Rhône to heavy barge traffic to the sea, and improving the drainage of adjacent agricultural land. In addition, the dredged material is being used to build port and industrial estates at Arles and Beaucaire.

The Petit Rhône is being dredged as far as Saint-Gilles, where a new large capacity lock will give access to the Canal du Rhône à Sète as a preparatory step to the modernization of that canal.

The C.N.R. has thus had a profound impact on the Lower Rhône area in a very short period of time, stabilizing existing activity through flood control, and paving the way for new developments in the form of port and industrial estates, power supply, irrigation, new river crossings, and recreational amenities. It is a crucial development in a sector of the Rhône valley which has thus far lacked a strong industrial stimulus. The success of the Donzère-Mondragon scheme suggests that an intensification of activity downstream is likely, especially once the Rhône is opened up to high-volume canal traffic, with pushed convoys of 3000 to 5000 tons moving up-river as far as Lyon by the close of the Sixth National Plan in 1976.

It is clear that the impact of the C.N.R. has been massive in the Rhône valley. From modest beginnings, concentrating primarily on energy production, it has now become a major agency for economic, environmental, and strategic planning. As the harnessing of power nears completion, interest is now turned to the related improvement of navigation from Fos to Lyon and Dijon, and in due course to the Rhine. The induced effects have already been substantial, but these may well seem slight compared with future developments once Fos-sur-Mer is fully operational and the Rhône becomes a true inter-regional and international waterway. A chain of industrial estates (existing, under construction, or planned) lines the Lower Rhône. Their future development may well be long-term, for Fos is clearly destined to absorb the region's heavy industrial growth in the near future, and the waterway's prime function will be one of transit. Nevertheless, the likelihood remains that the Rhône corridor as a whole will acquire much more industry than in the past, and that the Lower Rhône valley, thus far only lightly industrialized, will experience much greater activity in the course of the next decade.

Harnessing the Lower Durance

The controlled exploitation of the Durance valley bears certain resemblances to that of the Rhône described above, particularly the multi-purpose approach, but in some respects it has its own individuality. Whereas the overall control of the Lower Rhône will not be completed for several more years, the work in the Lower Durance had been completed by 1971.

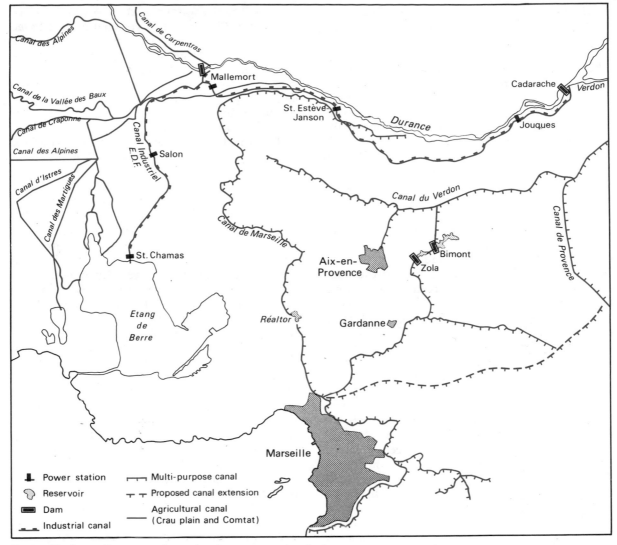

Fig. 5   The Lower Durance and associated water-control projects

The history of the Lower Durance valley is marked by a constant struggle to come to terms with the wayward character of the river. Uncontrolled, the Durance was a precious water resource and a constant threat to stable production. Deficient summer rainfall meant that water extracted from the Durance was vital to sustain irrigated agriculture, not only in the valley but throughout the Comtat Venaissin and on the margins of the Crau plain. As early as the twelfth century, irrigation canals siphoned water from the Durance, and by the nineteenth century a comprehensive network had been established and a complex organization brought into being to assure water distribution. However, the system was imperfect owing to the irregular seasonal régime: given the absence of effective storage,

the greater part of the annual discharge flowed unused into the Rhône. The lack of storage capacity was particularly crucial since the critical season for irrigation coincided with the period of lowest discharge. The Durance thus posed the double hazard of flooding in winter and spring and shortage of water during the period of maximum demand for irrigation. The uncontrolled nature of the river also meant a loss of potential energy, since both the total discharge and the valley gradient were advantageous for hydro-electricity generation. Small power stations had been built in the upper Durance valley early in the present century, but the bulk of the river's potential escaped untapped.

The problems of the Durance were the subject of research by a Development Commission after

World War II, and the decision to embark on a programme of integral development dates from 1955, with the nationalized electricity corporation responsible for the major engineering works. The key element was the construction of the Serre-Ponçon dam in the Upper Durance valley, completed in 1959. This created a vast artificial lake which permitted storage and thus complete control of the river régime, in turn permitting the construction of further power schemes in the Middle Durance valley between Serre-Ponçon and the confluence with the Verdon at Cadarache. Within the Lower Durance valley, the harnessing of the river has taken a highly individual form. Almost 90 per cent of the river's flow is diverted at Cadarache into an industrial canal on the southern flank of the valley which feeds the three power stations of Jouques, St. Estève-Janson, and Mallemort. At Mallemort the canal diverts the water southwards from its natural course and into the Etang de Berre, capitalizing on the increased gradient to drive two further power stations at Salon and St. Chamas. The harnessing of the Lower Durance for energy is thus complete, with an annual output of 2305 million kWh in total produced from the five stations.

This same control has permitted a more effective use of the river for irrigation, since the flow of water in the agricultural channels drawn from the now much-reduced Durance can be supplemented at will from the canal. The storage of water for hydro-electricity generation also ensures a secure position with respect to irrigation.

In addition to the developments within the Durance valley, the river also feeds the Canal de Marseille, supplying water to the agglomeration. The harnessing of the Durance has also paved the way for a more effective use of the Verdon. Water from the Verdon formerly supplemented the natural flow of the Durance but is no longer crucial. The exploitation of the Verdon water is entrusted to a mixed-economy company, la Société du Canal de Provence, which has already installed an irrigation system in the basins of Aix and Gardanne. The future use of the Verdon will benefit areas outside the Lower Rhône region, in the Var *département*, where an intensification of agriculture is envisaged. The harnessing of the Durance must be considered an outstanding technical achievement and one which successfully solves the problem, evoked in the preceding chapter, of the quest for environmental stability. The scheme has also brought considerable economic profit.

Agricultural modernization in Languedoc

The third example of a regional project based on hydrological development differs from both of those considered thus far, since it impinges much more directly on an established social and economic order. It is a project which attempts to solve the general problem of under-utilization of resources by raising the volume and value of output on the Languedoc plain.

This third project also extends well beyond the limits of the Lower Rhône region. The modernization of agriculture on the Languedoc plain has since 1955 been entrusted to the Compagnie Nationale d'Aménagement du Bas-Rhône–Languedoc (C.N.A.B.R.L.). Like the C.N.R., this is a mixed-economy development company in which Government and public organizations have a majority shareholding but which involves the private sector at the level of production. Its purpose is to modernize agriculture, primarily through the medium of irrigation, so as to diversify production, raise income levels, and break the monopoly of viticulture. The aim is not to eliminate viticulture, for in the areas of high-quality wine production, irrigation will be used to raise output and improve quality. However, a major objective is, by introducing a more varied and valuable range of crops, to reduce the area's concentration on low-quality viticulture that involves massive volumes of wine, the marketing of which requires subsidy. In particular the aim is to increase the area under fruit trees, market garden crops, and irrigated pasture, based on the most modern techniques of production. The primary construction task involves the creation of an irrigation network. This is fed throughout the eastern and central sectors by water diverted from the Rhône and in the western sectors by water stored in the Hérault and Orb basins. However, the activity of the company extends beyond irrigation to include the acquisition and consolidation of land, the building of new farms, agricultural research and advice, and the creation of marketing systems. In addition, the company is involved in promoting the food processing industry, essential to absorb the region's potentially huge output. The company also intervenes in the building industry in an attempt to renovate villages and promote new housing schemes. The objective is thus not simply one of modernizing and diversifying agriculture but of providing an entirely new, stable economy and pattern of settlement on a regional scale.

Such comprehensive and ambitious targets must be viewed in a long-term perspective, and progress thus far indicates elements of success and certain shortcomings. Most progress has been made on the physical task of constructing irrigation systems. The powerful Aristide-Dumont pumping station raises water from the Rhône to the Costières du Gard and across Languedoc towards Montpellier, and major reservoirs and siphons have been built in the Orb and Hérault basins. These irrigation works have been accompanied by a vast increase in the area under fruit and vegetables. On the other hand, there has been a distressing tendency in recent years for the region to produce a surplus of fresh fruit, especially of high-grade apples. It would be ironic if so much effort and investment should result only in a surplus of high-quality produce replacing one of low-quality wine. In part the surplus results from deficiencies in marketing and the inadequate development of the processing sector, and it results partly from market resistance in France to a product which although of high quality and attractively packaged, is expensive. This price problem applies particularly to apples, whilst peaches face competition from established peach-growing areas in Provence and the Rhône valley. For this vast enterprise to succeed in the long term, further improvements to the marketing and distribution network are called for, together with an expan-

sion of the fruit and vegetable processing industry. It is clear, too, that the potential output can be absorbed only on a European-scale market, which emphasizes the need to minimize production, packaging, and transport costs. The types of specialization must also be adjusted to real market demands.

Progress has not been evenly distributed throughout the Languedoc plain. The most impressive changes have occurred in the eastern sectors, which fall within the Lower Rhône region. This is due to several factors, of which access to the water of the Rhône is the most important. The Costières du Gard is a low plateau covered in fluvio-glacial debris, overlooking the low-lying littoral. It is not a naturally productive area, and large expanses lay fallow before the recent improvement. Moreover viticulture was here less extensive than further west on the Languedoc plain, and there was thus less resistance from an entrenched agricultural system. Once water was made available from the Rhône, the company was able to make rapid progress, and over 30 000 hectares are now irrigated in this sector, together with a further 20 000 hectares in the Montpellier district, outside the Lower Rhône region but also fed by the Rhône (Fig. 6). In the space of a decade, the output of fruit and vegetables in the Gard *département*

Fig. 6   Irrigation projects by the C.N.A.B.R.L.

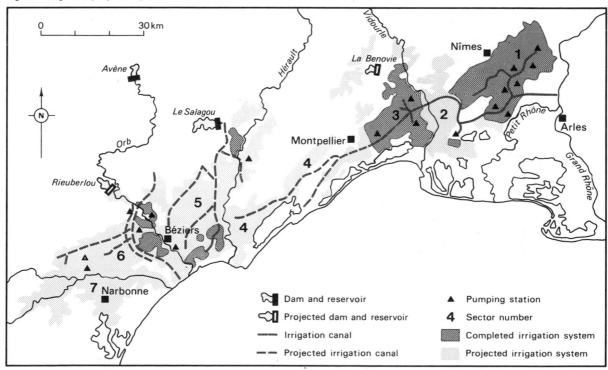

increased ten-fold, Nîmes developed as a major marketing centre, and an international processing company established a plant at Vauvert. Co-operative production and marketing has progressed rapidly, and the larger producers commonly work under contract to processing firms, although this intervention of 'foreign' capital is not universally appreciated.

The transformation of economy and landscape in the Costières du Gard has been profound, and one effect has been to draw this area more firmly into the orbit of the Lower Rhône region and away from the rest of Languedoc. Taken together with the successful construction of the Grande Motte tourist complex, described below, and the growing commercial and industrial importance of Nîmes, the activities of the C.N.A.B.R.L. have succeeded in their objective of raising economic levels in this marchland of Provence and Languedoc.

Coastal tourism west of the Rhône

As indicated in Chapter 1, the area immediately to the west of the Rhône delta extending as far

Fig. 7   The development of coastal tourism in Languedoc; (inset) La Grande Motte

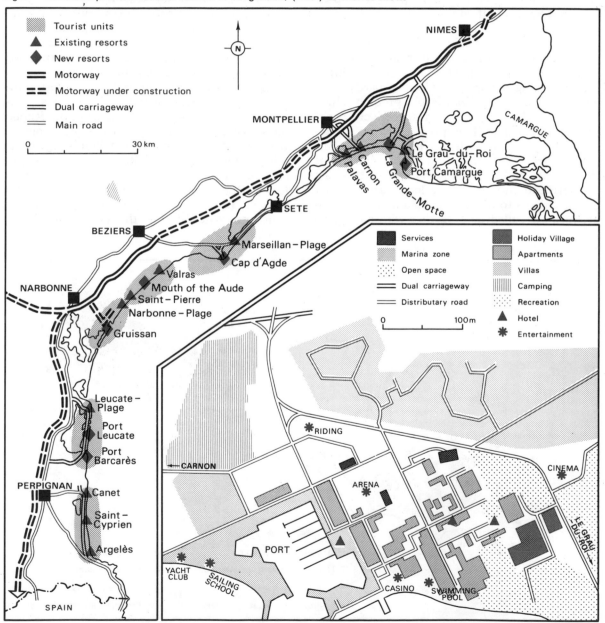

as the western limit of the Gard *département* is a zone of contact between the Lower Rhône region and the much larger geographical unit of the Bas-Languedoc plain. It therefore falls under the influence of planned developments in both these regions. Two major regional schemes are involved: the modernization of agriculture on the plain, described above, and the development of tourism on the coast. In principle, these are both projects conceived within the context of Languedoc, but both intrude geographically into the Lower Rhône region.

The Government decision, taken in 1963, to create new tourist complexes on the Languedoc coast arose from several considerations. In general terms, the great absolute expansion in holidaymaking in the 1950s, both by the French population and by foreign visitors, found France underequipped in terms of accommodation and facilities, and lagging behind competing nations such as Spain and Italy in the rate of new construction. This was a threat to France's traditional surplus of foreign exchange gained from tourism. Secondly, whereas the Côte d'Azur was becoming yearly more congested and expensive, the 200 kilometres of sandy coastline west of the Rhône lay virtually empty, resulting in a fundamental distortion of development on the Mediterranean littoral. Thirdly, the promotion of tourism was seen as part of the general need to improve communications, attract investment, and create new employment within the planning region of Languedoc. The specific causes of underdevelopment on the coast were the lack of roads in a zone punctuated by large lagoons and swampy marshes (and therefore of difficult access), mosquito infestation during the summer, and the deficiency of fresh water supplies.

The Government accordingly established an Inter-Ministerial Mission in 1963, backed by central funds, which proceeded to purchase large expanses of land and to delimit areas of controlled development. It was the task of this mission to prepare a detailed physical plan for the entire littoral, completed in 1964, and subsequently to direct its implementation. Six new tourist units were designated (Fig. 7), consisting of additions to existing small resorts and completely new complexes built on land acquired by the Government. A target capacity of 400 000 visitors was set, including 250 000 to be accommodated in the new complexes, together with moorings for 10 000 boats. In order to minimize the environmental impact that would have resulted from a motorway along the coast, the tourist units were to be linked by spurs to the main

inland motorway, and urban development between the units was to be restrained. Similarly, a programme of afforestation was to be started in the immediate hinterland, and the recreational use of the lagoons exploited under controls.

The implementation of the plan has been achieved under a three-tier administrative structure. The Inter-Ministerial Mission retained overall responsibility and was charged with the purchase of land and with the infrastructure developments requiring large amounts of investment and strong legal powers. The Mission thus created the land reserves for the new resorts and, in collaboration with the local authorities, built the dual carriageways for access, constructed the new ports, carried out the fly-eradication programme, and installed the fresh water supply. The task of laying out the new resorts was delegated to local Development Corporations of a mixed-economy nature, backed by Government and local funds and on a non-profit-making basis. The main responsibilities of the Development Corporations are thus the provision of local roads, parking areas, public recreational facilities, and basic urban services. The Corporations then sell the improved sites at cost price to the third tier in the construction process, the private commercial developers. The private sector is responsible for the final construction of apartments, hotels, villas, and commercial facilities. The buildings must conform to the official plan for the resort, but they may be sold on the open market.

The project is now well advanced. Priority was given to the two complexes of La Grande Motte and Leucate-Barcarès, both of which involve considerable new construction. The case of La Grande Motte is worthy of more detailed study since it lies within the Lower Rhône region.

La Grande Motte

La Grande Motte (Fig. 7) is the major new element in a tourist complex which groups the existing small resorts of Le Grau-du-Roi, Palavas, and the new marina settlement of Port Camargue. Construction of La Grande Motte began in 1965 with a target of accommodation for 42 000 persons and a mooring capacity for 1000 boats. The resort was inaugurated in 1967 with the new yacht basin and marina as its focus. Pyramidal apartment blocks give the resort a futuristic appearance. The ground floor of the pyramids is occupied by commercial establishments, and a high degree of separation of traffic from pedestrians is achieved. Surrounding the central apartment complex is an arc of camp sites, individual

villas, public open spaces, and recreational amenities, leading to holiday villages on the periphery of the resort.

In a very short period of time La Grande Motte has progressed from a building site to a virtual new town, equipped with a range of permanent services. The success of the complex is in part due to its ease of access following the construction of link carriageways to the inland motorway and the proximity of regional airports at Nîmes and Montpellier. To the west, the expansion of Carnon consists primarily of apartment construction, but to the east, the marina settlement of Port Camargue is entirely new and of striking conception. The new villas, built in the interior of the yacht basin, are accessible directly by boat.

La Grande Motte demonstrates the achievements of the regional project, in that an ultra-modern resort has been built and equipped very rapidly. Similar progress has been made at Leucate-Barcarès. However, in the last few years some slowing down has become apparent in the rate of construction, and with the abandonment of the projected unit based at the mouth of the Aude river, it seems certain that the plan for the littoral will not be completed in its entirety. This arises partly from the very high cost of the development and the inevitable diversion of both public funds and private investment from other coastal areas worthy of development, notably the Aquitaine coast. Secondly, in spite of stringent efforts, the element of speculation cannot be entirely eliminated. Speculation has taken place in both land and property. Land values have risen in the peripheral areas immediately adjacent to the controlled zones designated by the Mission. Similarly, the free sale of property

by the developers enables individuals to buy apartments primarily as a real-estate investment, resulting in artificially low occupancy rates, in turn predjudicing the commercial success of the resorts. The commercialization of the resorts has also created some regional opposition, since many of the transactions are in the hands of capitalists outside the region, some even from West Germany and Britain. Coupled with this is the fact that only a small amount of permanent employment is generated once the construction phase is completed. Nevertheless, the total number of visitors to the resorts has been increasing by over 10 per cent per annum over recent years; and the Inter-Ministerial Mission is to be wound up in 1975–6, by which time its task will have been completed.

As far as the Lower Rhône region is concerned, the principal effect of the project has been to intrude an entirely new landscape into the region in the form of the Grande Motte complex. However, the fact that this adjoins the protected zone of the Camargue Regional Park suggests that no further major eastward expansion of this particular form of development is likely in the future.

Planned developments in the Marseille Metropolitan Region

Whereas the planned developments so far considered concern well-defined geographical units with specific combinations of physical conditions, Marseille represents an entirely different spatial entity, that of a metropolitan region. The Marseille Metropolitan Planning Region is the area which looks to the city as an economic, commercial, and cultural focus, this being facilitated by a dense network of communications centring on Marseille. The region (Fig. 8) is thus a functional one, defined independently of physical boundaries although in detail profoundly affected by the nature of the terrain.

The Marseille Metropolitan Plan had its origin in the Government decision taken in the 1960s to prepare master plans for the long-term development of the major French agglomerations, including the *métropoles d'équilibre* designed to counterbalance the excessive weight of Paris, and a small number of other areas of major urbanization such as the Lower Seine valley. The master plan for the Marseille Metropolitan Region was published as a White Paper in 1969 and looks forward to the year 2000. The region covers 2800 square kilometres, the greater part of the *département* of Bouches-du-Rhône. In 1968 the region had a population of 1 350 000 which is expected to increase to 3 200 000, as an upper limit, by the year 2000. The plan is essentially a strategic one, indicating the broad lines of development considered desirable, and is summarized in Fig. 8. The plan does not incorporate detailed proposals and is subject to constant revision as circumstances change. The degree of precision is also highly variable as between the different zones of the region, in particular between the areas to the east and west of the Etang de Berre. In United Kingdom terms it is essentially a structure plan, designed to co-ordinate development on a rational long-term basis.

As far as the Marseille agglomeration is concerned, the plan recommends a strengthening of the city's regional role, consistent with its status as a *métropole d'équilibre* and compensating for the relative decline of traditional activity in port and processing industries. The main directions of growth are seen as being eastwards, along the Huveaune valley towards Aubagne, and north-eastwards on to the southern flank of the Chaîne de l'Etoile. Secondary commercial and industrial centres will need to be implanted in the agglomeration to ease congestion in the centre. The Chaîne de l'Etoile, the Iles Frioule, and the littoral within the agglomeration will be further developed for leisure activities, but the

Fig. 8   Major elements of the Marseille metropolitan structure plan

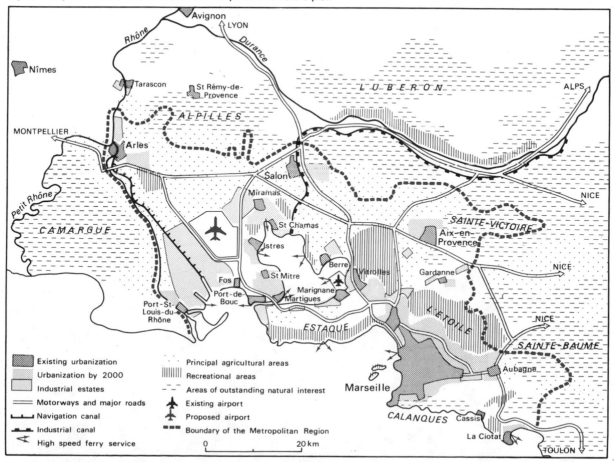

Calanques coast will continue to be protected. The present tourist functions of Cassis and the industrial activity of La Ciotat are expected to continue with but little change in the existing urban structure of these places.

Development inland from Marseille will continue to be based on the basins of Aix-en-Provence and Gardanne, surrounded by protected natural areas and high-value agricultural land. Aix-en-Provence has almost doubled in population in the last fifteen years, due to an expansion of its service and residential functions. The town's physical expansion is hindered by the shape of the Montagne–Sainte-Victoire area of outstanding natural attraction and by intensive irrigated agriculture. Its future expansion will be towards the north and west, and the acquisition of light, high-technology industry is desired to offset the present dependence on tertiary activity. The strategic position, commanding the Durance valley route to the Alps and the modern motorway to Nice and Italy, could aid this objective. The expansion of Gardanne beyond its existing industrial base and as an overspill area for Marseille is anticipated, coupled with the use of the Chaîne de l'Etoile as a recreational area.

The future development of the north-western sector of the Metropolitan Region is inevitably bound up with the growth of Arles. A relatively small and compact town, Arles has potential for expansion eastwards on to the Crau plain, and for industrial development northwards along the Rhône towards Tarascon. By contrast, the Chaîne de l'Estaque and the Côte Bleue, in the south of the region, are seen to comprise an outstanding area to be conserved for recreation. Whereas the proposals for the above zones are relatively precise, at least in terms of the available options, the Metropolitan Plan is much more reticent as to the future development of the area surrounding the Etang de Berre and extending across the Crau to the Rhône. This ambiguity stems from several considerations. In terms of available space this clearly constitutes the major area close to Marseille capable of absorbing large-scale development, whether based on existing centres or as new towns. However, the area already accommodates activities, notably aviation and petroleum refining, which generate large amounts of traffic and cause pollution problems. The construction of the port/industrial complex at Fos, offering the prospect of large-scale employment growth, and further traffic density and pollution, complicates an already difficult planning situation. It follows that the detailed physical planning of this zone requires a far more exhaustive analysis than was possible in the White Paper. The question of the impact of the Fos-sur-Mer project is so crucial that a description of its main outlines is necessary before returning to the problems of the future development of the Etang de Berre–Crau zone.

The site of the Fos port/industrial complex photographed at the construction stage   Port Autonome de Marseille

Supertankers discharging at the new petroleum terminal at Fos

Fos-sur-Mer

In a historical sense, Fos-sur-Mer represents simply the continued evolution of the port of Marseille. From its nucleus in the Vieux Port, the modern port has extended westwards by stages, involving first the construction of the artificial port, and after 1924, the specialized annexe of the Etang de Berre. Between 1948 and 1952 the role of the Etang de Berre was reinforced by the construction of the petroleum port of Lavéra. With the closure of the Suez Canal it was rapidly apparent that Lavéra was incapable of handling the new generation of supertankers built in response to the use of the Cape route. The Port Authority therefore turned its attention further westwards in 1960 to the Gulf of Fos with its favourable combination of deep water and adjacent level land. In addition to meeting the navigational requirements of larger tankers, the Fos site offered the opportunity of creating a port complex capable of restoring the fortunes of the

port of Marseille in competition with ports such as Genoa and Barcelona. The opportunity to create a complex not only of modern port facilities but also of related industries was seen in 1960 as essential to the long-term development of the port's activity, and in turn, to the industrial dynamism of the whole Marseille region. The timing of these proposals was propitious, since it coincided with the inception of Government policies in favour of a wider dispersion of industry benefiting particularly southern and western France. The idea of a strong growth pole in the Midi, in addition to solving the specific problems confronting Marseille, thus accorded with national planning priorities. This was a vital factor in the rapid approval, financing, and construction of the Fos project. In the longer term, Fos could also be seen as the southern terminal of an international Rhône–Rhine axis.

The choice of Fos was justified by its excellent qualifications. After dredging, the navigational conditions permitted the berthing of the largest vessels then contemplated. The absence of tides permitted docking at any time. The adjacent land of the Crau plain is level and easily excavated for dock construction, but at the same time firm enough to permit industrial building. There the project was not in competition with other forms of land use. Moreover, the site benefits from the completion of the other regional projects described above, in that a wealth of energy is available from the Rhône and Durance schemes whilst abundant fresh water is available from the Durance industrial canal. In addition, the completion of the Rhône navigation presents Fos with a deep inland waterway. Finally, in the Port of Marseille Authority, a ready-made administrative and operational body was available. These exceptional circumstances, coupled with Government encouragement, explain the very rapid evolution of the project. By 1961 the process of land acquisition had begun; in 1966 the Port of Marseille's development plan had been approved; and in 1968 the first stage of the port had been inaugurated, capable of receiving tankers of over 250 000 tonnes. At the same time, the Government decision to build a giant steelworks was announced.

The present outlines of the Fos project are summarized in Fig. 9. The port consists of two huge docks occupied by specialized berths for petroleum, bulk mineral, and container handling. Between these essentially industrial docks and the existing port of Port-Saint-Louis-du-Rhône, space has been reserved for a commercial port, which in itself will exceed the present capacity of the port of Marseille. At present the petroleum terminal, consisting of three berths, is in operation, supplying the Esso refinery at Fos completed in 1965, as well as the established refineries on the Etang de Berre. The mineral berth on Dock No. 1 is used for handling bauxite by the Pechiney Company for its refinery at Gardanne, and a container berth is in operation in Dock No. 2. A methane terminal is operated by Gaz de France handling liquefied natural gas from Algeria. In addition to the port facilities, the complex consists of a vast industrial zone of over 7000 hectares, of which 4500 are to be devoted to factories and over 2200 are already allocated. Fig. 9 indicates that the eastern section is devoted primarily to the reception, transfer, refining, and storage of petroleum and refined products. The central section is occupied by the steel industry consisting of the Société Lorraine

Fig. 9   The Fos-sur-Mer port/industrial complex

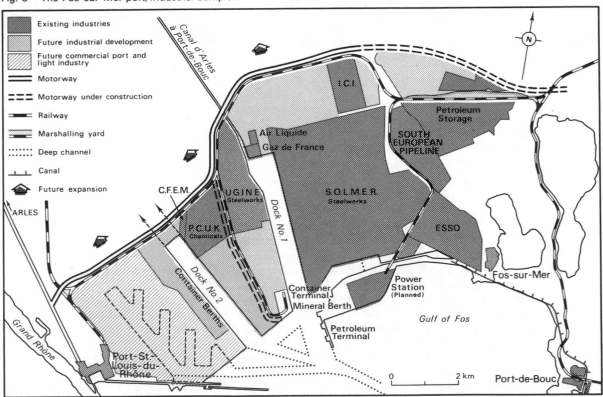

et Méridionale (S.O.L.M.E.R.) integrated iron and steel plant and the Ugine special steel works. The S.O.L.M.E.R. plant, inaugurated in 1973, is scheduled to be one of Europe's largest units, with an output of 3·5 million tonnes by the end of 1974 and an eventual capacity of 7 million tonnes. Output will consist primarily of sheet steel, and the mills will also roll the special steels produced in the Ugine plant. The two plants will ultimately employ over five thousand workers. Other major plants already in production include an I.C.I. factory, producing polyethylene, and Air Liquide, producing industrial gases. A total of over fifty firms were in operation or had reserved sites on the Fos estate at the end of 1973. The entire complex is served by a ring motorway and by rail, and the major firms operate their specialized berths in the port system. Moreoever, both the port and the industrial estate are capable of a vast extension northwards towards Arles, although the precise outlines and phasing of such an extension are at present undetermined.

In the space of a decade, the Fos complex has progressed from being Europe's biggest building site to being a well established industrial port. Thus far, Fos has met greater success as a port handling bulk commodities than as a growth pole

providing the kind of stimulus to industrial development within the region that the original port of Marseille failed to provide. Although a number of large firms have been attracted to Fos, they perpetuate the former pattern of processing industries. Moreover, the majority of smaller firms are in fact of a service rather than a manufacturing character. As yet only simple linkages between a small number of factories have developed, and after a decade of spectacular progress it seems likely that the future growth of the Fos complex will be more measured. The beneficial effects anticipated by many inland towns, in terms of a general stimulus to industrialization by virtue of their proximity to Fos, have proved to be over-optimistic, at least in the short term. In the immediate future it seems certain that the direct impact will be local rather than regional, but in the long term Fos will emerge as a growth pole for the Lower Rhône region as a whole. It is clear also that in the short term, the impact of problems engendered by Fos will continue to be on the immediate area, including the margins of the Etang de Berre. These problems include the effect of motorway construction and heavy traffic, pollution from heavy industry, and the need to provide housing for the permanent

The new S.O.L.M.E.R. steelworks while under construction at Fos   Port Autonome de Marseille

Urban expansion on the shores of the Etang de Berre at Martigues

labour force that is now replacing the temporary work-force living in shanty towns while involved in the construction stages.

To return to the context of the Metropolitan structure plan, it is obvious that the area around the Etang de Berre poses particular planning difficulties. A development as potentially massive as Fos introduces difficulties with regard to long-range planning since it is difficult to forecast population trends and the need for services. The task of planning the future development of the communes surrounding the Etang de Berre has been delegated to a specialized planning agency which is currently preparing detailed physical plans involving new town construction. Decision-making is complicated by the fragmentation of local government and the varying political affiliation of the communes involved. The prime source of investment for new urbanization will be the rates paid by firms operating at Fos, but the sharing of this revenue between the communes has involved delicate compromises. The three communes of Fos, Istres, and Miramas, politically linked to the Government majority party, are amalgamated as an inter-communal

group for new town development and the expansion here will consist of extensions to the existing settlements (Fig. 10). The three communes of Port-de-Bouc, Martigues, and St. Mitre, supporting the opposition parties, have also formed an association for new urban expansion. A separate town extension is to be built at Vitrolles, to the east of the Etang de Berre, although this will function more as an overspill for Marseille rather than absorbing the growth generated by the Fos project. These schemes are expected to absorb population growth in the immediate future; but should the upper limits of population projections be attained, then further urbanization will be necessary by the close of the century. Various strategies are being considered, but the most likely options are a completely new town on the Crau plain or major extensions to the existing towns of Arles and Salon. Above all the Etang de Berre zone offers the clearest example of the tendency for the speed of technological change to outpace that of progress in physical and social development. New motorways, port extensions, and industrial estates have mushroomed as a result of rapid decision-making in both the public and private sectors. The process of an accompanying planned urbanization has proved much more difficult.

Planning in the Marseille agglomeration

The strategic plan for the Marseille–Berre Metropolitan Region is concerned with establishing long-term guidelines. Meanwhile, the agglomeration of Marseille itself wrestles with day to day problems of a more specific character and demanding immediate attention. These problems have already been described: the movement of industry to sites outside the agglomeration, a similar trend with respect to port development, the loss of colonial trade exacerbated by the closure of Suez, the physical decay of large sectors of the city, the need to rehouse large numbers of immigrants, the need to reduce the transport strangulation imposed alike by the physical constraints of the site and the central location of much employment, and the need to enhance the directional role of Marseille in the tertiary sector to offset the increasing port and industrial functions of Fos. City planning therefore embraces the problems of housing, transport, employment, and urban renewal.

The problem of transport is particularly acute since the two major employment concentrations, the central business district and the port zone, are situated at the heart of the agglomeration, whereas new suburbs progressively mount the surrounding mountains. An increasing separation of place of residence from place of employment is taking place, augmenting the volume of

Fig. 10   Industry and urbanization around the Etang de Berre

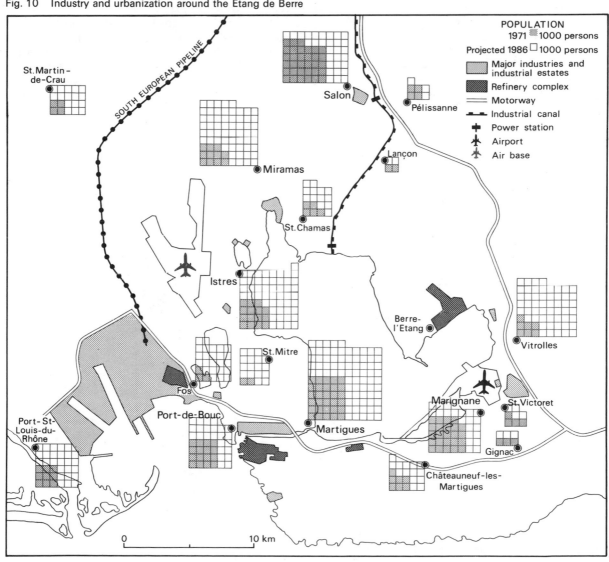

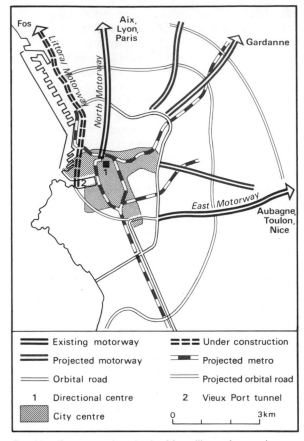

Fig. 11 Transport plans in the Marseille agglomeration

arteries to dual-carriageway standard is virtually complete. Given the physical constraints of the site and the extremely dense building pattern, motorway and carriageway construction can be only a slow and expensive solution.

Furthermore, new roads themselves add to the problems of congestion and parking. Accordingly an underground railway system is planned and work began on the first line in 1974. This first line will run from the port area to the city centre and beyond to the southern suburbs. A second line is envisaged as a loop linking the eastern and north-eastern suburbs to the centre. When completed, the metro system should make for improved travel within the central zone and easier commuting from the main suburban zones. In theory at least, the transport plan should reduce congestion by the separation of different types of traffic at present in a state of conflict.

The plans to improve the housing and environmental quality of the agglomeration are equally ambitious. Six comprehensive development areas (*zones d'action concertée*) have been designated which are planned to include 18 000 dwelling units and provide employment for 7000 workers. In particular this should permit the rehousing of the large immigrant population at present living in shanty towns or in overcrowded areas of the old

Fig. 12 City-centre redevelopment in the Marseille agglomeration

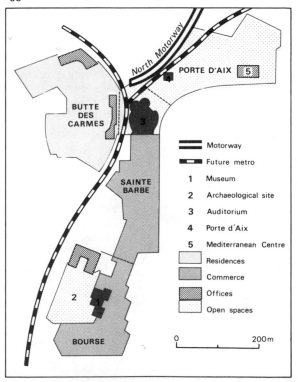

commuting within the agglomeration, to which must be added the very high density of goods-vehicle traffic needing to reach the city centre and the large number of daily commuters from outside the agglomeration proper. The situation is exacerbated by the fact that of all French cities, Marseille has one of the highest proportions of private car users in its commuting population.

Marseille is already served by two motorways which penetrate to the city centre: the northern motorway, in effect the Paris–Lyon–Marseille motorway, and the eastern motorway to Aubagne. The current transport plan envisages the provision of further access motorways (Fig. 11); and the littoral motorway, joining Fos to the port of Marseille, is already under construction, penetrating the port area as an elevated expressway linking up with the road tunnel under the Vieux Port. The motorways will be intersected by a series of three orbital roads linking the suburbs with the centre and also acting as bypass roads for through traffic. The first of these, consisting of an improvement of existing urban

City-centre redevelopment in Marseille: new commercial blocks replace decayed housing. In the centre, the archaeological remains of the Greek settlement

city that are ripe for redevelopment. A further measure designed to improve the urban environment is the creation of a major recreational zone on the Prado beach to the south of the agglomeration and on the offshore islands. However, the most spectacular exercise in renovation concerns the city centre. A large section of central Marseille, extending from the Vieux Port to the Gare St. Charles is scheduled for redevelopment. The first stage of this city centre renewal is now being undertaken (Fig. 12), and it emphasizes the link between transport, and employment, and housing policies. The scheme is seen as creating a *Centre Directionnel* in the heart of Marseille, accommodating commercial and cultural functions appropriate to Marseille's status as a *métropole d'équilibre* within France and as a major commercial port and city in the Mediterranean world. Emphasizing this latter role is the planned

Mediterranean International Trade Centre, a tower block housing the offices and data bank of a commercial institution intended to establish Marseille as a hub of Mediterranean trading. The first stage is divided into four parts (Fig. 12). The Bourse sector will be devoted to commercial and office use while preserving the recently discovered remains of the original Greek settlement and providing a museum. This is prolonged by the Sainte-Barbe sector devoted primarily to commerce but also including a new auditorium. The Butte des Carmes sector will predominantly comprise housing, but will also include social amenities, shops, and offices. Finally, the Porte d'Aix sector will consist of gardens surrounding the Port d'Aix monument, a sports centre, and, dominating the entire project, the tower of the Mediterranean International Trade Centre. In total it is planned that 7000 persons will live in this

41

A *manade* of wild bulls grazing in the traditional Camargue

French Government Tourist Office

Directional Centre, 18 000 will work there, and 65 000 persons will visit it daily. It will be served by metro and by motorway to Marseille airport, and it is situated between the port and the main-line railway station.

While seemingly an ambitious project, the *Centre Directionnel* is in fact a measure of the scale of urban renewal that Marseille requires. Although some piecemeal renewal was achieved in the form of post-war reconstruction, particularly around the Vieux Port, the backlog of renewal in the city centre is considerable. It is of significance also that the task of renewal is being combined with an effort to enhance Marseille as a focus of service activity, balancing the industrial and port attraction of Fos, and that, deprived of an important hinterland, the city is attempting to project its influence outwards into the Mediterranean world as a whole.

The Camargue Regional Park

Whereas the projects described so far have as their principal objectives the encouragement of development, this final example of planned activity is concerned with containment and limitation of economic growth. The Camargue is an area of outstanding natural and scientific interest which is experiencing pressures from all sides and from within. Its designation as a regional park is intended to preserve its natural attributes whilst at the same time permitting a controlled use of its agricultural and tourist potential.

The Camargue may be subdivided into four generalized landscapes (Fig. 13) corresponding with different patterns of resource use. A broad arc surrounding the northern margins, broadening markedly on its eastern limb adjacent to the Grand Rhône, constitutes the agricultural Camargue. It is a zone of alluvial soils deposited by the two branches of the river, irrigated from this same source, and devoted to rice cultivation and, to a lesser extent, to vines and orchards. The town of Arles forms the natural marketing and processing centre for this zone.

Secondly, the heart of the Camargue consists of two large nature reserves coinciding with the vast Etang de Vaccarès and the adjacent communicating lagoons to the west. The two reserves form in effect a single protected zone of 13 000 hectares, maintained in a natural state, the habitat of rare bird species and the nesting ground of pink flamingos. The Natural Zoological and Botanical

Reserve occupies 10 000 hectares of lagoon, salt-marsh, and woodland. It was created in 1928 when the Pechiney Chemical Company loaned it for 75 years to the National Nature Protection Society. The second reserve, of 3000 hectares surrounding the Etang dit l'Impérial, was acquired by the *département* of the Bouches-du-Rhône in 1964. Together, these two reserves constitute a core area of the Camargue within which public circulation is strictly controlled and access is extended primarily to research workers.

Between these two landscapes, the former entirely artificial and the latter in its natural state, extends a broad but discontinuous zone which, while more or less in a natural condition, is in private ownership and is the scene of some economic activity. The landscape consists of alternating saltmarsh, shallow lagoons, and halophitic scrub. It is a zone of bull- and horse-rearing on large estates overlooked by horseback 'guardians'. This is the traditional Camargue, sought after by tourists. In addition to the free grazing of herds of wild bulls (*manades*), large areas are left in a natural condition as shooting and fishing reserves for the proprietors. Economic activity consists of animal rearing and supporting the tourist industry by providing bulls for the local arenas and horses for the increasingly popular trekking. It is a zone increasingly penetrated by 'second home' construction and by tourist amenities. The area nevertheless plays a vital role in the overall ecological balance of the Camargue, as a feeding and breeding ground for wildlife and in stabilizing hydrological conditions. It follows that any change in the function of this zone not only destroys the traditional Camargue, already much reduced in extent, but also compromises the natural balance in the protected reserves.

The final section of the Camargue forms an extension of the above zone but has a more specific function. The south-eastern corner is devoted to the salt industry, based on Salin-de-Giraud. This is the largest marine salt producing district

Fig. 13   The Camargue Regional Park

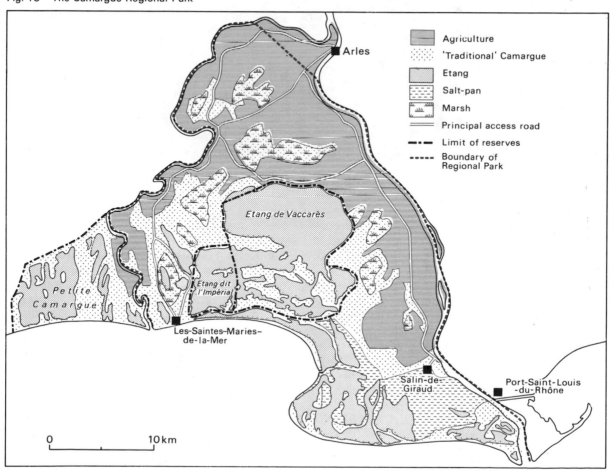

French Government Tourist Office

The Camargue is a complex of natural and artificial hydrological features. Here a channel (*grau*) connects a salt lagoon with the sea

in Europe, with vast areas devoted to the concentration basins and salt pans. Although a semi-industrial land use, this activity, too, preserves large areas for wildlife.

The pressures exerted on the Camargue are strong and increasing. External pressures include the urban development of Arles and to a lesser extent of Les-Saintes-Maries-de-la-Mer, the expansion eastwards of tourism on the Languedoc coast, the creation of the Fos complex with its threat of industrial pollution, and the ever-increasing tide of tourists, for the most part circulating by private car. Internal pressures result from the conflict between the varying land uses. The post-war expansion of the agricultural zone has not only reduced the area of the traditional Camargue, but has modified hydrological

conditions, whilst the use of chemical fertilizers, weed- and insect-killers alters the chemical composition of the water and threatens the wildlife habitat in the reserves. The traditional zone is also under pressure from the tourist influx (which includes over 600 000 visitors per annum to Les-Saintes-Maries-de-la-Mer alone), from *ad hoc* second home construction, and from uncontrolled camping on the beaches. The preservation of the wildlife, natural landscape, and traditional character of the Camargue thus demands a reconciliation of land uses between the contrasted zones, a measure virtually impossible before the creation of the Regional Park with appropriate legal and financial powers.

The Camargue Regional Park was officially constituted in 1972, its direction being in the hands of a Foundation representing public and private interests. The Foundation combines national, regional, and local government authorities; the nature reserve trust; the salt industry; and representatives of property holders in the Camargue. It has specific tasks and objectives as the directional and administrative authority for the Park. Some priority is accorded to research into wildlife and botanical conditions.

The management of the Park is based on a zoning principle, particularly as concerns freedom of public access and development permission. A zone of wildlife protection has been designated coinciding with the reserves which it is planned to extend by purchase of additional land and by contract arrangements with landowners. Access to the reserves will continue to be strictly controlled. A second zone, of limited public access, is to be created in certain areas which, whether in a natural or agricultural state, can support a limited amount of tourism. A third zone, coinciding with the main public access roads and the littoral, is to be open to the public without restriction, but with improved facilities and a stricter control over car traffic.

A further policy is to support those activities which enhance the landscape and assist the preservation of wildlife, and particularly to support the traditional activities threatened with decline. This policy involves ensuring the survival of local breeds of bulls and horses; aiding the maintenance of a rich folklore, expressed in traditional fêtes and pilgrimages; and establishing open air museums. The Foundation is also interested in protecting outstanding buildings and archaeological sites. In addition to these broad policies, the Foundation intends to intervene over a large range of relevant issues, from the monitoring of pollution in the Rhône to the substitution of underground cables for the existing surface electricity and telephone lines.

The total area of the Regional Park is 82 000 hectares and the population of 8000 inhabitants has declined steadily in recent decades. Agriculture accounts for over 60 per cent of all employment. In principle, an area of such size with a very low population density and, apart from salt extraction, a virtual absence of industry, appears eminently suitable for successful operation as a park. In practice the position is far from straightforward. Many of the pressures are exerted from outside the park and are therefore beyond the jurisdiction of the Foundation. Secondly, although the park is very extensive, access is via a very limited network of roads and the problems of localized pressure inevitably result. The size of the park also presents problems of finance, if comprehensive improvement is to be carried out. The purchase of land to enlarge the reserves is particularly expensive. Finally, the very fact that the controlling authority includes all the vested interests in the area makes for policy difficulties because of the conflict of interests involved.

Although the notion of a Camargue Park has existed for over fifty years, it is still in its infancy as a reality. Many difficulties and obstacles remain but at least there is now an awareness of the threat to one of the last remaining areas of unspoilt lowland in southern France and the worst abuses should in future be avoided.

4 Towards 2000—The Grand Delta

The six projects described in the preceding chapter illustrate the strategic position of the Lower Rhône region at the hub of planned regional development in the French Midi. Of necessity these projects were summarized individually, but in reality they clearly have an impact on each other and also on the areas adjacent to the Lower Rhône region. It is increasingly recognized that in order to find rational solutions to development problems, the whole of south-east France must be regarded as a single unit, although no formal administrative or planning framework exists to correspond with this reality. It has been left to spontaneous unofficial initiative to point the way to a strategy entitled 'the Grand Delta'. The Association for the Grand Delta was founded in 1966 on the initiative of businessmen and public figures and has rapidly emerged as an influential movement uniting the three planning regions of Provence–Côte d'Azur, Languedoc, and Rhône–Alpes—which are linked by the Rhône spine. This unit embraces one-fifth of the national land area and has ten million inhabitants, including the nation's second and third largest agglomerations. The basic aim of the Association is to promote the expansion of the Grand Delta as a counterbalance to the heavily industrialized Rhine delta region and to rival the growing industrial strength of northern Italy. The Association brings together representatives of industry, commerce, public administration, and professional organizations, who are able to influence policies and decisions at the highest level in order to achieve a concerted approach to development in the Grand Delta. The movement has gained tacit Government approval of its approach to regional strategy. The decision to create Fos as not merely an annexe to the port of Marseille, but on a scale capable of serving the whole of the Grand Delta, accords with the Association's conception of south-east France as a region of potential European significance. The concept of the Grand Delta requires that metropolitan and industrial structures, together with their supporting infrastructures, must continue to be built on a European scale, and much has already been achieved in this direction. The Fos port/industrial complex, the South European Pipeline, the hydroelectric development of the Rhône and Durance, the Paris–Lyon–Marseille motorway and the canalization of the Rhône are all examples of inter-regional development which promote the integration of the Grand Delta. The theme of this volume therefore contrasts markedly with that of many others in the *Problem Regions of Europe* series, which describe the attempt to revitalize and restructure old, established regions. Activities in the Lower Rhône region point the way to the still more ambitious attempt to speed the birth of an entirely new regional entity, deliberately conceived in a European context and at the scale of an enlarged European Community.

Further Work

This volume has attempted to analyse the broad patterns of development in the Lower Rhône region, and detail has been confined to the discussion of recent trends and planned intervention. The background physical geography and the character of the cultural landscape therefore form an essential field for further reading. The basic physical and human outlines are summarized in:

Monkhouse, F. J., *A Regional Geography of Western Europe*, Fourth Edition (Longman, London, 1974).

Houston, J. M., *The Western Mediterranean World* (Longman, London, 1964), Chapter 20.

A discussion of development problems in the area is contained in:

Thompson, I. B., *Modern France, A Social and Economic Geography* (Butterworth, London, 1970).

Clout, H. D., *The Geography of Post-War France* (Pergamon, Oxford, 1972).

The same problems are described in more summary form in:

George, P., *France, A Geographical Study* (Martin Robertson, 1973).

Scargill D. I., *Economic Geography of France* (Macmillan, London 1968).

Further detailed information on specific topics is contained in the following articles:

Agnew, S., 'The Vine in Bas-Languedoc', *Geographical Review* (1946), p. 67.

—, 'Rural Settlement in the Coastal Plain of Bas-Languedoc', *Geography* (1946), p. 65.

—, 'The Cultural Heritage of Bas-Languedoc', *Geography* (1951), p. 44.

Clout, H. D., 'Expansion Projects for French Seaports', *Tijdschrift voor Economische en Sociale Geografie* (1968), p. 271.

Graves, N. J., 'Une Californie Française—the Languedoc and Lower Rhône Irrigation Project', *Geography* (1965), p. 71.

Hoyle, B. S., 'The Etang de Berre: recent port expansion and associated industrial development at Marseilles', *Tijdschrift voor Economische en Sociale Geografie* (1960), p. 57.

—, 'Changes in the Durance Valley', *Geography* (1960), p. 110.

Jones, I. E., 'The Development of the Rhône', *Geography* (1969), p. 446.

Lamour, P., 'Land and Water Development in Southern France', in *Comparisons in Resource Management* (Johns Hopkins, 1961), p. 234.

Manasseh, A., 'Changes in the Lower Durance Region', *Geography* (1973), p. 250.

Pilkington, R., 'Joining the Rhine and the Rhône', *Geographical Magazine*, 39, (1966), p. 214.

Thurston, H., 'France Finds a New Holiday Coast', *Geographical Magazine*, 41 (1968), p. 339.

In addition to the above references in English, the magazine series *Découvrir La France*, published by Larousse, is an extremely valuable source. Volumes 65, 66, 68, 71, 72, 73, 74, and 75 cover the region, and in addition to text contain a wealth of colour illustrations, maps, and diagrams.

Map coverage

A detailed topographic map coverage is provided by the *Carte de France*, 1:100 00 series, sheets Marseille, Aix, Arles, Nîmes, Montpellier, Carpentras, and Orange. A more generalized outline is provided by the 1:250 000 series, Marseille sheet. An equally useful, up-to-date, and less expensive coverage is provided by the *Michelin Carte de France* series at a scale of 1:200 000. Although basically road maps, this series contains generalized relief, canal systems, power stations, and major industries. The region is covered by sheets 80, 81, 83, and 84. Sheet 84, of the Marseille agglomeration, Etang de Berre, and Lower Durance valley, is particularly useful for classwork. The whole of the Lower Rhône region is very strikingly portrayed in the *Michelin* 1:200 000 tourist edition sheet of Provence.

Index